A BOY CALLED
COMBUSTION

A BOY CALLED COMBUSTION

GROWING UP IN 1940S MISSISSIPPI

BILL KEETON, MD

TO ASHLEY —
THAT YOU FOR ALL THAT
YOU DO FOR ME & PCA!
YOU ARE THE BEST!
BEST WISHES,
Bill
MARCH 2014

DEDICATION

In memory of my mother and father, William Brewer Keeton and Emily Fondren Keeton. With her never-ending and unconditional love, her total devotion to family, and her willingness to take on any task, Mother was the glue that held us together and the spark that kept us going. As a child, I thought there was nothing that my father could not do; now that I am an adult, that opinion remains remarkably intact. His talents, ingenuity, determination, and honesty knew no bounds. Yet he was always humble, and never lost his sense of humor or the twinkle in his eye.

To my siblings Gladys, Mary Agnes, and Richard, who despite my antics never gave up on me.

To Dee, my wife, "soul mate," lover, and very best friend. Despite her obviously poor taste in men, Dee is one of the most remarkable people I have ever known. I sincerely hope I can keep her fooled for a few more years, or at least until it is time for me to be dropped off at the Pleasant Pastures for the Elderly and Hopelessly Demented.

To my wonderful children and best friends, Anne, Beth, and Molly, and my truly incredible grandchildren, William, Cat, Audrey, and Emily, who make everything worthwhile.

Contents

A Forewarning,
in lieu of a Foreword

by Ken Goodrich

The photograph is a black-and-white, grainy 3x3 taken at a family gathering on a summer afternoon in Jackson, Mississippi. The picture shows a father, mother, and son in the shaded foreground of a huge pecan tree with dozens of other folk milling and conversing around them, almost every one of whom is eating from a paper plate piled ridiculously high with food.

The father, in a white, short-sleeved shirt open at the collar and dark trousers, a glass of (probably) iced tea in one hand and a smoldering cigarette between the fingers of the other, is standing slightly to the side of his wife. She has on a floral-patterned dress and is sitting in an Adirondack chair with her arms wrapped tightly around the torso of a short-cropped, black-haired boy outfitted in his own short-sleeved white shirt that is half-tucked in and half splayed out of his shorts. His dark socks, stuck into shoes with the laces untied, droop just below two visibly scabbed knees.

The father, a ruggedly handsome, solidly built man with a head of hair to die for—even though it appeared to be prematurely graying—is gazing either absent-mindedly or, more likely, with his inventive mind at full imaginative throttle, off to the left with a perfunctory for-the-photographer half-smile on his thin lips. The mother, a pleasant but—what is it, haggard?—looking woman with a kind but—what is it, strained?—face, is sort of smiling at the camera, but with gritted teeth. Her tension derives, apparently, from the Herculean effort she is exerting holding on to her obviously squirming son, who, although he has managed to slide off his mother's lap far enough that his shoes have found the welcome earth of promised escape beneath him, is, nevertheless, trapped under his armpits in the determined and well-practiced grip of his mother. As a matter of fact, if you look closely at the photograph you can tell how much the toned muscles of those upper arms of the boy's mother seem out of proportion to the rest of her soft, cushiony frame.

The year is 1945. The father and mother are Bill and Em Keeton. The son is Billy, otherwise known by everyone in the neighborhood, among other appropriately but affectionately bestowed monikers, as Combustion. All those folks surrounding them are the seeming cast-of-thousands, the extended gang of the Fondren family, which established the little hamlet that still bears the family's name about two or three miles north of Jackson's state capitol building along the main drag that is North State Street.

Today Fondren is one of the "chic" localities in Jackson, with trendy shops, restaurants, and watering holes, with which most of the whole city is familiar. And yet, I would be stunned if a handful knows its quaint, pure Americana history. Fondren was first a family, then a neighborhood, and then, in the burgeoning aftermath years of the war, a community. During the author's childhood of the 40s and early 50s, long before the theme song from the popular television series *Cheers* coined the phrase, it was a place where everybody knows your name. Neighbors blocks away, shopkeepers, the mailman, soda jerks, milk deliverers, gas station attendants, grocery store bag-boys: all knew who you were and whose you were.

It was a time and place when we kids as young as five years old banged out the kitchen door after breakfast, reappeared for lunch, and then took off once more, not to be seen again until either suppertime or dark, whichever came first, and our parents didn't necessarily know where we were or with whom or what we were up to. What they *did* know, and never gave a moment's thought to, was that wherever and with whoever the hell we were, we were safe. Neighborhood Watch was an innate way of life back then, rather than a sign-posted-against-strangers' warning.

And so it came to pass that into such a time and place, and to that expansive Fondren clan, of whom his mother was a second-generation sister of eight, William Frederick Keeton was not so much born as he exploded. His father's "William" was Bill, so, naturally, the son's "William" either had to be Billy or Fred. But by the time the little peckerwood could run amuck (having bypassed the learning-to-walk phase because, early on, he saw no point in *plodding* from Point A to every other point in the alphabet) it was clearly evident to his older sister, his parents, and his huge extended family of aunts, uncles, and cousins, almost all of whom lived within a half-mile square few blocks of each other in the reaching shadows of the ancestral home, the Big House—not to mention the remaining communal citizens who were *not* his family—that this Nor'easter of a kid was no "Fred."

That "Little Billy Wild Child" somehow survived to tell these wickedly delightful tales on himself is a remarkable testament to the deep well of love and long road of perseverance from his parents, but that he would grow up to pursue a career in medicine is not all *that* surprising. The foundation of medicine, like every other scientific field, is its incessant pursuit to discover and experiment with cause and effect. By the age of four, *this* kid caused every manner of previously unimaginable effects all over Fondren, Mississippi.

And so, *that* kid, the author of the book that follows, is Dr. William Keeton, an esteemed anesthesiologist and pain consultant in the vaunted medical community of Atlanta. His thinning but still wavy white hair curls roguishly over his ears and along the back of his collar. His youthful face belies his 72 years, with wire-rimmed glasses lending distinction to a pair of piercing eyes that are somehow both deadly serious and at the same time invitingly playful, almost always with an after-all-these-years glint of mischief in them. He is, without a doubt and almost incomparably, one of the most entertainingly humorous creatures on the planet....or, as he might put it, at least South of Memphis.

It is my privilege to be one of his many cousins, and, because of our ten years' age difference, it is a blessing upon my heart and soul to have come to know him so much better in these, our later years. What you are about to read are tales of a time and place long gone by. We who were Fondrens were so rich for having lived there and then, even as we are so poor that we cannot live it still.

One, final, somber, deeply-thought-out, and sensitive note about what follows in this too-long-delayed piece of work by the piece of work that is *Combustion*: You cannot make this stuff up.

Ken Goodrich
May, 2013

Sunday Dinner at the Big House

*T*HE DAY I RAN MY GRANDFATHER'S 1935 PLYMOUTH DOWN the gravel driveway and through the back of the garage started off like every other Sunday. After church, as always, we all went to the Big House for Sunday dinner. The Big House was my Fondren grandparents' home, not the state prison. It sat at the corner of North State Street and Fondren Place, two blocks north of my grandfather's grocery store. In Jackson, Mississippi, the names Fondren and the Big House were almost synonymous; people in town rarely mentioned one in a sentence without the other.

The Big House was a fourteen-room house with a large kitchen, dining room, living room, parlor, pantry, six bedrooms, a sleeping porch, and two bathrooms. The doors to the Big House were never locked, and all could come and go as they pleased. In addition to a constant stream of folks drifting in and out, a number of family members lived in the house over time.

Despite this, it was a warm and happy place. Other than some bickering between some of the children, I never remember an unkind word being spoken in this home. This is saying something, given that since the Big House was the gathering place of a large family, an awful

1

lot of words were spoken there. It still astonishes me that you could get so many people—including six brothers-in-law—inside a single house so often and have so few words of conflict or dispute. As a boy, I apparently found such peacefulness boring, so I did my level best to infuse the Big House, and Jackson generally, with some necessary excitement. But more on that later.

As I said, the Fondrens were a large family. Granddaddy Fondren and his wife, Annie, whom I never heard called anything but "Gran," had eleven children in all. Two girls and one boy died in early childhood, leaving seven years between the older five children and the last three. With the birth of David in 1904 the family seemed complete, with five girls and their one son. But in 1911 the Fondren begat machine cranked up again and spit out three more girls.

Nancy, who was the mother of my cousin and close pal Ann Mayberry: Emily, who was my Mama; and Dee were the three youngest. Amazingly, Nancy was born on the same day and in the same room in which her three-year-old sister died with diphtheria. Granddaddy called these last three girls—Nancy, my mother, Emily, and Dee—his "Trash Gang," stating that all they ever got was hand-me-down clothes, toys and dolls from their older sisters. But everyone agreed that what these last three lacked in worldly possessions was more than made up for by the extra affection they received from their parents, their adoring four older sisters, and their brother David.

The household was rounded out by two black (or "colored," as we said then) ladies who were felt to be members of the family: Liza Miller, the cleaning lady, and Lee Robbins, who my father always said was the best cook he had ever known. This was quite a statement since to my mind *all* ladies at that time, black and white, seemed to be excellent cooks. In those days we ate real food, cooked on real stoves. Biscuits were made by mixing flour, lard, and buttermilk in a mixing bowl, rolling them out with a rolling pin, cutting out inch- and-a-half circles and baking them in the oven. There was none of this whacking a cylindrical container on the side of the counter and throwing the contents into a toaster oven for two minutes. There were no freezers. Heck, there weren't even refrigerators. We had iceboxes, and the iceman delivered a block of ice every day.

The Fondrens were a very close-knit family. Daddy said you did not have to be married to a Fondren very long before you found out you'd best not get into a disagreement with one of them unless you were willing to take on all of them. He said they were "thicker than thieves" and that the only thing that kept them from being a clan was that none of them knew diddlysquat about making moonshine.

One of the best things about growing up in the Fondren family was there were so many things you could depend on. I knew, for instance, that there would be at least 350 people in the Big House on Christmas morning. That may be a slight exaggeration and, Lord knows, if Mama told me once not to exaggerate, she told me a million times. I also knew that there would be scores of people coming from as far away as Edwards, Canton, and Lorenz Street (ten miles away, twenty miles away, and two blocks away, respectively) to the Big House for Sunday dinner.

Another thing that I could depend on was being in church anytime the doors were open. This, of course, was long before paid babysitters were commonplace. The only way other than school that Mama could get rid of me for a few hours was to send me to church. She sent me to Sunday school, Sunday morning church services, Sunday evening church services, League (the Presbyterian Sunday evening youth program), prayer meeting on Wednesday nights, choir practice, Boy Scout meetings, catechism class, and communicants' class. I think Mama may have been reprimanded for trying to send me to the weekly deacon's meeting on Sunday night and the women's circle meeting on Wednesday morning. When you think about it, all my time at church gave Mama a lot of time off. I wonder what the heck she did with it?

I could also depend on Mama knowing anytime I did anything wrong anywhere in town. That was because everybody in town either was a Fondren, used to be a Fondren, or wanted to be a Fondren. The information superhighway had nothing on this town. The lag time between something happening and everyone knowing about it was probably less than twenty seconds. When I arrived home after one of my frequent transgressions, Mama would be standing at the door with her hands on her hips, saying, "Billy Keeton, what have you been doing?" I knew "I was had" and would immediately think, *Oh, shit!* No, no, Mama, I'm just teasing. I didn't really think that. I would never have thought anything like that, honest! Cross my heart and hope to… well, never mind.

There were other things I could depend on, too. I knew every morning when I got up that I would be getting at least twelve spankings by the time I went to bed that night. Mama would, of course, do most of them, but there were plenty of aunts, uncles, grandparents, school teachers, maids, bus drivers, butchers, bakers, and candlestick makers around to pick up the slack anytime Mama was too busy or just "plumb wore out."

This particular Sunday started out like always, with the family gathered for dinner at the Big House. In the South of the 1940s, dinner was the noon meal and supper was "what got ate" in the evening. (I think "lunch" was something that was eaten north of Memphis, but I'm not sure anyone in Mississippi knew anything about it.) Dinner was substantial, while supper usually consisted of something like "cold 'coon and collards" and a glass of buttermilk, or maybe a bowl of clabber and cornbread. Clabber is what you get when you put a large bowl of milk out on the back porch and let it sit for a few days. First it sours, and then later it takes on sort of a greenish color and forms curds. At that point it is pronounced clabber and feasted upon. Now, between you and me, clabber is revolting stuff that would gag a maggot. But obviously I can't admit that for fear of not being looked upon as a pure Southerner. Which I most certainly damn sure am.

That day, Lee, Gran, and all of Gran's daughters were in the kitchen busily preparing the huge meal. Granddaddy and all of the men were standing around the kitchen, screen porch and driveway, smoking cigarettes and teasing each other unmercifully. They were telling jokes and carrying on, waiting patiently for their meal, and being careful to contribute absolutely nothing to the process of actually making it.

Because there was a twenty-one year gap between Ella, my oldest aunt, and Dee, my youngest, there was also a wide age span between the cousins. On this day in 1944, Betty Ann was sixteen. Martha Ann, Little Margaret, Little Marion and Sonny were around twenty. Gladys, my older sister, and my cousin Dave were ten years old. Gladys and Dave were together, as always, and the older girl cousins were helping in the kitchen. Sonny was busy helping the men smoke cigarettes and do nothing. In other words, you would think that there were enough people around to prevent what was about to happen, but somehow even those numbers didn't stop it.

With all the women working like crazy in the kitchen and all the men busily avoiding helping out, no one was paying much attention to Ann and me. My cousin, Ann Mayberry, and I were four and five years old, respectively, at that time. Ann was my constant companion and my best friend. As bad as I was, and as much grief as I gave everyone else, Ann and I never had a cross word between us. She was as good as I was bad. She was frequently a witness to my antics, but she never participated in any of them or tattled on me.

Even at that tender age I was already known to various uncles by nicknames such as Combustion, Cyclone, Roughhouse, Tornado, the Destroyer, and Little Billy Wild Boy. Uncle Fritz, known as Honey for reasons I can't explain, said I was easy to find: Just follow the sound of breaking glass or look in the "Hoorah Patch." Going to the Hoorah Patch was a Fondren-family euphemism for getting a spanking. And indeed, the Hoorah Patch was a place in which I spent much of my time. As one might guess from this, not paying attention to me was never a good idea.

Ann and I were playing in the yard when I suggested that we get inside "Flatfoot." Flatfoot was Granddaddy's 1935 Plymouth, named for a popular Sam Gaillard song called "Flat Foot Floogie with a Floy Floy." Yeah, I know. But it makes at least as much sense as "When the moon hits your eye like a big pizza pie, that's *amore.*"

I don't remember ever seeing Granddaddy drive this car—he walked to work at the Fondren store, which was only a few blocks away—but it was always sitting in the driveway, waiting for whoever might need it. Not everyone had a car back then. My father didn't buy his first car until he was thirty-seven years old. But even though most people in the family did not have a car, Flatfoot was rarely used. City buses and walking were the main sources of transportation.

Once I had convinced Ann to get in Flatfoot, we took turns playing like we were driving. Of course at that age our feet didn't reach the pedals, and we couldn't see out of the windshield unless we were on our knees in the driver's seat. When it was Ann's turn to pretend to drive, she got busy "steering." I told her that I would get down on the floor and work the foot pedals. I did it just like I had seen the adults do, alternating between pushing the accelerator, the brake, and the clutch. To my mind this driving stuff seemed pretty easy. There really wasn't much to it. If I had just had a cigarette hanging out the corner of my mouth, I bet I would have looked just like Daddy did when he was driving a car. Then I reached around and moved the gearshift—I had seen adults do that, too. That's when Ann started screaming. I suddenly realized that the car was moving. It was probably thirty to forty feet from the garage, which was slightly downhill from where Flatfoot had been parked. I jumped up from the floor and watched wide-eyed as the car moved downhill with ever-increasing speed.

The garage was actually a shed with two sides and a back wall. Open across the front and wide enough for two cars, it had a roof supported by two wooden 4x4s down the center. Flatfoot was headed straight for the center of those 4x4s. Cars in those days were made out of real steel. By the time Flatfoot reached the garage it had enough momentum to go easily not only through the 4x4s but right out through the back of the shed. With the center supports and part of the back wall now missing, the garage roof sagged all the way down to the point where it was actually touching the top of Flatfoot. I'm not sure why it didn't totally collapse.

At the sound of the crash, pandemonium spread rapidly throughout the Big House. Within seconds, it seemed like every adult that Ann and I had ever known was screaming, running toward us, and desperately trying to get the doors of the car open. They were all so relieved that neither of us was injured that we were not punished. Quite the contrary. Instead, Lee and the women admonished the men, who had stood idly by while two innocent (a word that was seldom used to describe me) children got into the car unsupervised. I heard Lee say "Lawd, you gotta watch that Billy ever second, if'n you 'spect this house ta still be standin'! I love that chile, an' he don't mean no harm, honest he don't, but dey ain't nuttin' he can't tore up in less 'an a minute, if'n he ain't watched ever second!"

As the head of the family, Granddaddy had the last word. "The children are alright, the car looks okay, and the garage can be fixed, so let's eat," he finally said. Everyone agreed, so we all filed into the dining room.

The dining room had the expandable drop-leaf table needed to seat such a large group, which was covered with a lace tablecloth, the good china, crystal, and silver. Granddaddy and Gran sat at either end, and their eight children and spouses sat around the table with the older cousins. To sit at the big table you had to either shave or wear a brassiere. Four of us—Dave, Gladys, Ann, and me—did not qualify by either of these criteria. For us there was a card table. It wasn't far from the big table but it did not have china or crystal. We had everyday plates, and we drank from jelly glasses. At that time jelly came in glass containers with a metal top. After the jelly was finished, the container was washed and used as a six-ounce glass. While our table settings weren't as pristine as those at the big table, we shared the same food and all the love in the room.

That Sunday in 1944, World War II was in full force. Dee's husband, Fritz, was in the Army Air Corps. Sonny, Aunt Ag's oldest son, had just joined the Marines. Both were soon to go overseas. As the dinner table discussion began to focus on the fact that it might be a long time before we were all together again, Granddaddy decided that we needed to have a photographer take a picture. Daddy said he knew just the person to do it. He jumped up and called the man, who came right over.

Everyone was there except Aunt Bob. This aunt, whose name was actually Ella, was married to Granddaddy's only son, David, who was called Snooks. Aunt Bob should not to be confused with Uncle Bob, who was married to Aunt Margaret. If you knew them you would probably never make that mistake. Uncle Bob was bald and always had a shirt pocket full of pencils, cigars, and extra eyeglasses. Aunt Bob, on the other hand, had lots of hair and rarely smoked cigars. Aunt Bob had not come to dinner that Sunday, because she had the flu. Since she lived just across the street, however, she could be quickly summoned. She was told to get out of bed and get dressed immediately. She reluctantly obeyed, and we assembled on the front steps for the picture.

Photos were still taken with film back then, and film wasn't even made in lightproof rolls yet. Loading and unloading the camera had to be done in the dark. The photographer ducked under the black cloth hood of his camera and got everything lined up. Before the man could take the picture, Granddaddy yelled, "Wait a minute Somebody go get Lee! We can't have a family picture without Lee!" Lee was even more reluctant to be photographed than Aunt Bob, but with gentle coaxing she finally came out. Liza certainly would have been included as well, but she did not work on Sundays and no one would have intruded on her day off, even for that momentous photograph.

After the picture, the family reconvened in the dining room for dessert. I had gone ahead of the crowd to investigate what was always my favorite part of the meal. On the kitchen table rested two large, beautiful pies. Each pie was covered with meringue, which was peaked and delicately browned. They were gorgeous! But the meringue made it impossible to tell what kind of pies they were. Lee, who knew how much I loved chocolate, teased me that both pies were lemon, which she knew I did not like at all.

I stood on a stool carefully inspecting the pies, putting my elbows on the table on either side. Resting my head on my hands, I looked ever so closely for any sign of chocolate around the edges. As I did my inspection, my hand slipped and my face went directly into the pie. Sure enough, it was chocolate, but no one other than me seemed very interested in eating it by then.

Lee constantly tried to protect me from the much-deserved trips to the Hoorah Patch that I made on a daily basis. She would say, "Now, Miss Em, he didn't go to do it." Although she was rarely successful in these interventions, this time it worked. I think that was partly because the family was still relieved that Ann and I had not been obliterated when Flatfoot crashed through the garage, and partly because I must have been a pretty sad sight, crying and with my face completely covered with chocolate and meringue. But, between you and me, that pie was delicious … and I had it all to myself.

Mama

*M*AMA SAID IT WASN'T THAT I WAS BAD, EXACTLY—IT WAS just that I had the "dickens" in me. I was never quite sure what a "dickens" was, but everyone agreed I had more than my share of whatever it was. This was a real problem, but Mama and the rest of the family knew just how to deal with it.

In 1940s Mississippi, child discipline was a matter of the highest priority. To spank or not to spank wasn't yet the question that it later became. The question was only who would administer the discipline and what method would be used. Spankings were usually done by parents, but others, including aunts, uncles, teachers, maids, postmen, travelling salesmen, and anyone else who happened to be passing by, were also permitted to carry out this task any time it was necessary. The methods included, but were not limited to, bare hands, rolled up newspapers, Ping-Pong paddles, rulers, brushes, and belts. If you grew up in a different time, place, or family than I did, that list might sound pretty scary. But in the way they were visited on me, none of these methods inflicted any damage, and most didn't even cause any significant pain. Spanking was more an act of intimidation than anything else, and the effect was pretty much the same whether a paddle or a powder puff was used.

Mama had a theory that if you "whooped" a kid for the first few years of his life, you could slack off after that. Mind you, she didn't express it quite in those terms. Her phrasing would have been something like, "If you raise a child properly and exercise firm discipline appropriately, then he will have a keen sense of discernment for the path of righteousness in later life." Mama always did have a way with words. But like I say, loosely translated, that still came down to "If you whoop 'em early on, then the little brats will finally shape up."

The theory certainly held up well as far as my goody-goody older sister was concerned. I think it only took one spanking when she was two, and the promise of another when she was five, to "whip her into shape for life." She never did get into any trouble. Can you imagine what it's like, for somebody like me, to come along behind a sibling like that? To make matters worse, my younger sister was practically as saintly as my older one. Her idea of fun was to sit in the corner and play with her little dolls. Always happy, she never got into any trouble either. Boring, gutless, and inscrutably unimaginative, if you ask me.

When it came to raising me, Mama started out applying her theory as planned. At the start she had no idea of the enormity of her task. She surely never realized that "whipping me into shape" was going to be a sixteen-hour-a-day job, though it didn't take her long to wise up. At the beginning, she was determined to make something—anything—out of me. Later she decided to make the best of it, even though she was convinced there must have been a mix-up at the hospital nursery. How else could she explain the difference between my precious sisters and me? She couldn't think of anything she had done to make God that mad.

Eventually, she lowered her expectations to a more realistic level. She decided if she could just keep me out of Sing Sing, she would forfeit the rest of her dreams. In fact, at one point I think she even thought that the state pen wouldn't be so bad if she could just keep my picture off the post office walls.

Even after she lowered her expectations, the job wasn't easy. It required a lot of stamina to administer, say, twelve spankings a day. It also required some ingenuity to keep them from getting monotonous. She employed the versatile arsenal mentioned above on a daily basis and eventually added shoes, coat hangers, broom handles, and tire tools. Okay, maybe that's a little exaggeration. Exaggeration always does make the story better.

But the worst of all had to be the switch. Switches were produced by removing a long, thin branch from a bush. Then, carefully, one by one, each leaf would be removed while the victim watched nervously. What remained was a long, thin, whip-like instrument. While this did not cause any lasting damage, it produced a definite sting when it struck bare skin. It wasn't by accident that there were numerous suitable switch bushes around Mama's house.

When I had been really bad, I would be commanded to go outside and pick my own switch. Now *that* is cruel and unusual punishment. I mean, would you make a condemned man put the rope around his own neck or strap himself into the electric chair? Of course not! The Supreme Court wouldn't stand for it. Well, let me tell you, picking your own switch is worse. Especially when you consider that the child asked to do so might be just a sweet, innocent little cherub like yours truly.

Naturally, I couldn't do even this simple task without sometimes getting into mischief. One time when Mama sent me outside to pick my own switch, I decided that I would make it as easy on myself as possible. This led me to pick a tiny little twig three or four inches long. When I gave it to my mother, her eyes narrowed and her mouth tightened into a little circle. In a slow, purposely controlled voice, she told me to go get a proper switch or I was really going to "get it!" Her tone was instantly recognizable as one that even the Terminator wouldn't mess with.

Returning to the yard drenched in self-pity, I looked for an especially large switch in the hopes of making her feel guilty. Then a wonderful idea struck me. Instead of picking a switch, why not take her the large limb that had recently fallen from the walnut tree? That baby was a good three to four inches in diameter and five to six feet long. Literally dragging this into the kitchen, I offered it to Mama. She immediately sat down, put her head on the breakfast table and sobbed pitifully. Chalk one up for the home team! Not only was there not a switching, there were hugs, kisses, and great admonitions of never-ending love. I think she completely overlooked the next three to four transgressions, too.

But, alas, all good things must come to an end. Eventually, Mama was able to shed her guilt. One day she invited me once again to pick my own switch. No problem; the code had been cracked. I went straight out into the yard and quickly returned with a log. That was when I first learned what it means to "overplay a hand." This time she darn near used the thing on me.

Poor ol' Mama! She never did really spank me after I was six years old. That probably had more to do with her being "plumb give out" than my being "whipped into shape."

Either way, she certainly deserved better than she got. Mama probably really was the only thing that stood between me and a career at Sing Sing. But I honestly don't think it was the spankings that kept me out. It had a lot more to do with the love that she gave than the discipline she dispensed. The truth was that if twelve spankings were given in a day, twenty were deserved. And there was never a day when the hugs didn't outnumber the spankings at least three to one. Mama made me constantly aware that while she didn't approve of my behavior (hell, nobody did), she very much approved of *me*.

Day in and day out, she comforted my every hurt. She would take me on her lap, tell me stories like "Goldilocks and the Three Bears" and "Little Red Riding Hood," or recite nursery rhymes until the tears were gone. At night she would read from a book of Bible stories for children—Joseph and his many-colored robe was my favorite. She always had time to play with me when I was lonely, which was fairly frequently, as most of the neighborhood avoided me like the plague.

Mama was, and is, the closest thing to an angel I have ever seen on this earth: an angel in a homemade dress and an apron splattered with flour and stuck with sewing needles, already threaded and ready to be used for the next, inevitable rip, tear, or worn patch.

Although given every reason not to do so, Mama loved me from the bottom of her heart. There was never any doubt about that … even when she sent me outside to pick my own switch.

Daddy

THERE WAS ABSOLUTELY NOTHING MY DADDY COULDN'T DO. HE could easily beat up any other daddy in the neighborhood, **or all of them at once.** He could fly airplanes, tame wild animals, and wrestle alligators. He could have easily whipped the Japanese and Germans singlehandedly if they had just let him in the Army. All of this is true and without equivocation. You have my word on it.

I idolized my father from the day I was born. Until I was six years old, most of my sentences began with "Me and my Daddy." He was my best pal. I could not wait for him to get home each afternoon. I waited impatiently on the front steps until I saw Daddy approaching, and then jumped into his outstretched arms. We spent each evening together in the back yard until it got dark. We played horse and rider with him on all fours, hide and seek, or baseball. He never seemed too tired or too busy to spend time with me.

My father was full of energy, always doing something. He got up at 4:30 each morning, and after making coffee he served Mama a cup in bed. He then awakened my older sister and me with coffee too. Our version consisted of one part coffee, twenty parts milk, and two teaspoons of sugar. He then ate breakfast and rode the bus to work, returning around 5 p.m. to give Mama a much-needed rest from her obstreperous son. After supper he worked in his workshop until 11:30 p.m. With this schedule, it is a wonder any of us were ever conceived.

On Sunday afternoons, Mama and Daddy always took a nap. It wasn't until many years later that I understood why adults were always so sleepy on Sunday afternoons. When he emerged from the bedroom afterwards, he probably had a silly little grin on his face, though I didn't notice that at the time.

The rest of the afternoon would be all mine. Many of my favorite childhood memories are centered on those Sunday afternoons. We went to the zoo, the park, the train station and the airport. At that time there was only a four-foot-high cyclone fence between us and the airplanes. We didn't go to the movies or go swimming. Both of these activities cost money (being city folks, we did not have the luxury of free rivers or lakes), and it wasn't considered acceptable to do anything on the Sabbath that cost money. Anything involving cards or dice was also forbidden, even playing Old Maid or Monopoly. But despite those restrictions there was plenty of leeway for Daddy and me to have a good time.

The railroad yard was only a few blocks from our home, and we frequently went there on Sunday afternoons. We walked among the trains and visited the roundhouse, an amazing building at the end of the line. When the huge locomotives pulled into the building, the section under the train would turn 180 degrees so the engine could leave facing the opposite direction. Since in the 1940s of my childhood people hardly had windshield wipers on their cars, having a building large enough to contain and pivot a locomotive seemed to be quite a feat.

One day when we were walking among the trains, Daddy flagged down an engine as it came slowly down one of the side tracks. When he asked if we could go for a ride, the nice engineer seemed happy to oblige. *Hot diggity dog!* I can't remember ever being more excited. I almost knocked the engineer and fireman down getting on that engine and jumping up into the "driver's seat." The kind engineer let me wear his cap, ring the bell, blow the whistle and sit on his lap while pretending to drive the train. I was having the time of my young life.

Then he asked if I wanted to see what was behind the fire door. "Yes, sir!" I said quickly. I got as close as I could while the fireman opened the firebox. As he pulled the lever, the door flew open with a thunderously loud noise. There seemed to be ten thousand hells inside. The fire was raging, the heat was intense, the steam was bellowing, and I was suddenly acutely aware that I wanted to be anywhere in the world but there. I almost knocked down the engineer and fireman again as I made a mad dash to get off of that locomotive as fast as possible. Daddy chased after me while looking over his shoulder, waving and yelling "thank you" to the engineer.

Even as bad as I was, I received very few spankings from my father. This wasn't because he could not bring himself to do the frequently needed disciplining, but rather because with him a promise was as good as the real thing. He only needed to give me that certain look of displeasure and I immediately shaped up. I knew, without any shadow of doubt, that if he was telling me to get off of that chair, he not only meant now, but *right* now. I also knew that if I did not respond obediently, there would be "Hell to pay" without a moment's hesitation.

Daddy kept the key to his workshop on a hickory stick about fourteen inches long so that he wouldn't lose it. This workshop key hung over the kitchen door and, much to my dismay, had other uses than merely opening locks. It was my father's primary instrument of discipline. The mere mentioning of "the workshop key" brought on a complete change in my attitude. I lived in fear of that stick until the age of five, when I decided to take matters into my own hands and do away with it entirely. I climbed up on the counter, removed the stick and threw it, key and all, down the storm drain in front of the house. For some unknown reason, Daddy did not replace it. Maybe he was relieved not to have to use it that way any more. I never had to worry about that method of discipline again.

Key stick or not, there was never any change in the deep respect that I had for him. I feared him, but I idolized him at the same time. This seems like a paradox, but over the years I have continued to observe that the parents, teachers, coaches, and so on who command the most respect are frequently also the most loved.

I have never known anyone to work as hard or as long, with as much total commitment, no matter what the project. It didn't matter whether he was working on his latest invention or something trivial like building a house for the neighbor's dog. He was an absolute perfectionist in everything he did. He had a zeal for finding a better way of doing just about everything, and a gift for doing it that led him to patent multiple inventions. Watching Daddy work on them, I learned just what Thomas Edison meant when he said, "Genius is two percent inspiration and ninety-eight percent perspiration."

While selling automotive equipment, my father got the idea for the bumper jack. It sold nationwide—just about every service station and tire store in the land had at least one of them. Later, when he went into the picture framing business, he revolutionized the whole industry, improving the way frames were made and developing a foolproof new mat cutter.

Stating that he had little use for school, my father had dropped out after the eighth grade. Despite this, he spoke perfect English and had impeccable manners. I don't ever remember him reading a book for pleasure, but he researched the things he was interested in thoroughly, mostly mechanical and engineering problems. I can't help but wonder what he could have done as a mechanical engineer or an orthopedic surgeon. (For more on my father's inventions, see *Afterword: The Frame Shop*.)

Daddy was also a natural salesman. At one time or another he sold tire handling equipment, picture frame supplies, stocks and bonds, and even hearing aids. I was twelve years old when he was selling hearing aids to the older rural citizens of southern Mississippi. It was then that he told me something I have never forgotten. "When someone asks you how you are, do *not* tell them," he said with total sincerity and some disgust, looking me straight in the eye. "I can assure you, they are just being polite by asking. They do *not* really want to know. Believe me, there is nothing worse than actually being told all a person's ills and burdens. Just say you are fine and dandy, whether you are or not."

Ever since then, I've been fascinated by the negative replies given to the simple greeting "How are you today?" Responses vary from "Tolerable" to "Terrible" and from "Okay, I guess" to "I'll be better at five o'clock." As Daddy said, a simple "Great, thank you; I hope you are well too" seems so much wiser, even if you do have an inflamed hemorrhoid!

My father could be gruff at times, but was gentle and honest to a fault. He always said, "If you tell the truth, then you will never have any problem remembering what you said." He was always busy. But however busy or absorbed in a project, there was always time for his family. Family always came first.

And he was never too busy to help someone. Daddy loved people; he was as interested in the porter or shoeshine boy at the train station as the governor or president. Color was no bar for him. Even though he was raised in Mississippi by parents who were tendentious (to say the least) where race was concerned, Daddy couldn't see a problem with having a black person sit next to you on a bus, drink out of the same water fountain, or swim in the same swimming pool. This was a very liberal view for someone of his time and place, and I have always respected him greatly for that—as I do for virtually everything else.

In many ways I don't seem much like my father. I went to school forever rather than dropping out. I am medical by inclination, and while I am fairly mechanical, I'm not in his genius range. He was a highly talented and accomplished musician and I barely have enough rhythm to walk. He was well organized, orderly, and prompt in all he did; nobody has ever accused me of being organized, and procrastinate is one of the things I do best. But I hope I'm like him where it counts, and if I die being half the man that he was, I'll count my days fulfilled. To me, that's what "daddy" means—a friend to enjoy, a teacher to learn from, a mentor to look up to for life. And my Daddy more than lived up to the name.

Granddaddy Fondren

*M*Y GREAT-GRANDFATHER, RICHARD FONDREN, MADE HIS way to Jackson, Mississippi, from South Carolina as a young man. I'm not sure what this says about my family heritage, since I think South Carolina is where the English sent all of their prisoners and ne'er-do-wells. In 1845, Richard purchased a 485-acre plantation north of Jackson. There is a lot of rich farming soil in Mississippi, but I think Richard and his family soon realized that none of it was in, or even around, Jackson.

His youngest son—my granddaddy, David—decided against farming, attending business college in Jackson instead. He then bought a small lot, located where North State Street and Old Canton Road came together, from Isham Cade, a former slave. He built a wood-framed general store called D. F. Fondren's General Merchandise and Fancy Foods in the area known as "Sylum," so named because the Mississippi Insane Asylum had been located in that area in 1855. He may have thought this would be convenient for visiting some of the relatives that no one ever mentioned.

Whenever I asked about my ancestors, I was told we were Scotch-Irish. That seems like an interesting combination when you think about it, given that the two groups haven't always gotten along too well. Sort of like being an Arab-Israeli, I guess.

Granddaddy died when I was only five, but I remember him vividly. My memories include him standing at the grocery store's counter in seersucker pants, out by the chicken coop, and standing at the Christmas tree, giving out presents on Christmas morning. In my memories, he was always smiling, happy, kind, and gentle. From everything I've ever heard, including the stories about him I've been told all my life, I'd guess that is a pretty accurate recollection.

With eleven children, Granddaddy Fondren probably figured that owning a grocery store was the only way everybody would get to eat. Just a couple of blocks north of the store, he built the Big House for all that gang of his. It would be convenient to have it so close—he probably guessed that he would be his own best customer.

The store was the center of the Fondren community (downtown Jackson was three miles away). The local post office was housed there. Granddaddy was postmaster general, as well as the grocer, butcher, stock boy, and the guy who cleaned the windows and swept the floors. The post office was listed as Fondren, Mississippi. Fondren Presbyterian Church started as Sunday school in Granddaddy's living room. He served as a deacon in the church for many years. Although asked on many occasions, he never served as an elder, saying he wasn't worthy.

Granddaddy Fondren was a good businessman and knew how to turn a profit. He was also extremely honest and fair. I developed an early bent toward entrepreneurship as well. In the beginning, however, I sort of forgot about the part where you were supposed to be honest and fair.

Actually, if I do say so myself, I developed a couple of pretty slick little schemes. If Granddaddy had just left me alone, I'd probably be rich right now.

Like all the best plans, my first scheme was simple. Under the grocery store counter were little brown paper bags that were used for small purchases such as penny candy, spools of thread, snuff, and the like. As

I looked at these small bags one day, it dawned on me that they were exactly like the ones the street vendors used to sell peanuts.

Geez! I could make a fortune!, I thought. Or at least enough money to pick up a few Hershey bars and a Dr. Pepper®, anyway.

I pilfered a few bags when no eyes were on me—not easy, since there were very few times when there weren't a lot of eyes on me. Taking them out beside the store to the gravel driveway, I filled them with small rocks. Carefully twisting the ends so they looked like bags of peanuts, I began selling them to my grandfather's customers as they left the store. The price was only ten cents and the contents were so delicious they were guaranteed to bring tears to your eyes—especially if you bit down on one of them.

At first, things were going great. The money was rolling in. Easy Street was just around the corner. Whoever said that crime didn't pay?

Then my Sunday school teacher discovered the true contents of her bag and felt duty bound to inform Granddaddy. That woman never did like me.

Located near the back of the store, Granddaddy Fondren's office consisted of a desk and a safe. I don't remember what all was said when we convened there, but I think we discussed honor, integrity, and what George Washington, Roy Rogers and Jesus would have done in similar circumstances. I also think that Granddaddy suggested that I sit in the corner by the safe until I had had sufficient time to ponder the magnitude of my sins.

I'm ashamed to say that it was during this time of repentance that my next scheme was developed. This was long before I had read any self-help books suggesting turning stumbling blocks into stepping stones, but instinct told me I must not be sidetracked by this small setback.

In those days, the glass bottles that held beverages like Coca-Cola carried a two-cent deposit. Enterprising young men (and some old ones too, for that matter) collected bottles that had been discarded on the side of the road and returned them to the store to collect the money.

Granddaddy kept the returned bottles stacked behind the store until they were picked up by the bottling company.

Now, trudging around in the hot Mississippi sun, finding the bottles and then carrying them back to the store was a lot of work, not to mention very time-consuming. But it didn't take much effort at all to pick up a few bottles behind the store, where they were already neatly stacked, and carry them to the front counter. Boy, was Granddaddy pleased to see me on such an industrious path after my less-than-admirable start in the business world! As he counted my pennies he seemed to glow with pride.

He seemed somewhat less pleased as I approached the counter the second time. By the third time I strolled up with an armload of bottles, it was painfully obvious that he had caught on. Once again, I don't remember exactly what was said or done in our trip to his office. But I do remember quite well that my next time in the corner was, of necessity, spent standing.

Even though he sometimes had to play the disciplinarian role, Granddaddy Fondren knew how to be a boy's buddy. Once, after tearing through the store, upsetting displays of stacked cans, knocking over drink bottles and tripping an elderly customer, Mama commanded me to sit absolutely still on a box in the center of the sales floor. She made it clear that my neck would be broken in six places if I so much as moved a little finger or made a single sound. As I sat there in front of all those people, totally embarrassed, Granddaddy pulled a box alongside of the one I was sitting on. Neither of us said a word. He just sat there with me, sharing my shame and punishment, making it lighter and easier to bear.

One of the reasons for our closeness might have been that Granddaddy was pretty starved for boyish companionship. Out of all those children he only had one son, and I was the only grandson who lived in Jackson. Luckily for me, he not only liked little boys, he liked *bad* little boys. I've been reminded a thousand times that Granddaddy used to say, "Billy's much to my liking. There's enough spit in his eye to make me crazy about him." I've never tired of hearing that. It's still the kind of special bond that makes this boy proud.

Paint, 1

*A*S BEST AS A FOUR-YEAR OLD COULD TELL, THE GENTLEMAN painting the screen porch at the Big House was a real professional. His name was Mr. Harrison. He was using a brush that was four inches wide to paint molding that was only two inches wide. I found this absolutely fascinating and asked many questions. I had planned to be a telephone pole climber when I grew up, but now house painting seemed to be a better choice.

Mr. Harrison showed me how he handled the brush, seeming pleased that I appreciated his workmanship. He also showed me how to feather it in such a way as to not get any paint on the screen while painting the narrow molding. He seemed to do this with little effort. "Nothing to it, really, once you get the hang of it," he said with a cigarette hanging from the corner of his mouth.

I continued to watch Mr. Harrison until it was time for his next break. Painting the thin molding took a good deal of dexterity. It was clearly not something that could be done while rolling a cigarette. I had seen a lot of people who could roll a cigarette with one hand, but not while painting two-inch molding with a four-inch brush. So Mr. Harrison took a break to have his next smoke.

It is, I suppose, conceivable that he may have wanted to enjoy a brief escape from his young apprentice. But I didn't worry about that. While he was gone seemed like the perfect time to practice the skills he had so patiently shown me. I knew that it would be a real treat for him to realize that his work had progressed even in his absence.

With an imaginary smoke hanging from the corner of my mouth, I explained what I was doing in great detail to Jackie, my imaginary playmate. I deftly dipped the wide brush into the paint. Only after it started dripping paint all over the floor did I remember the part about wiping the brush gently on the side of the can to remove the excess paint. Oh, well. That was just a small and insignificant detail. It would soon be overshadowed by the finesse I would demonstrate in painting the remainder of the porch, a task I figured should only take a few minutes.

Seeing the four-inch paint glide over the slightly less than two-inch molding, I recalled something Mr. Harrison had said about turning the brush sideways so as to keep the paint off the screen. However, I sort of liked the painted-screen effect, so I painted several more screens just like it.

Boy, is Mr. Harrison ever going to be excited when he gets back and sees all the work I've done!, I told Jackie. Actually, I had no idea just how excited he would be. Come to think of it, I may not have ever seen anybody as excited as he was.

Mr. Harrison became even more excited when he realized that I had also painted the left rear fender of my Uncle Snooks's Pontiac. The unique effect predated the popularity of two-tone cars. As I recall, Uncle Snooks wasn't as appreciative as one might expect with having the very first black Pontiac with a white fender in the entire city of Jackson.

My work left poor Mr. Harrison faced with two options, neither of which was very appealing. He could take the blame for the drippy floor and painted screens. Then again, Granddaddy might not believe him. Even the worst of painters wouldn't have managed to get paint on a nearby car.

Or, he could tell my grandfather what a brat his grandson was. While I doubt that Mr. Harrison did much future painting at the Big House, Granddaddy seemed to understand his predicament.

I've said it before: despite the trouble such episodes caused my grandfather, he seemed to get a kick out of the fact that I was, as he said, "a real pistol." I think he couldn't really scold me this time around because he was too busy laughing.

Mama, on the other hand, did not seem to have any trouble whatsoever controlling her amusement. I don't think she laughed again for at least a month. She might have chuckled again about the next time I was able to sit down without a cushion. She obviously was trying to discourage my career as a painter, but there would be battles yet to come over my fascination with paint.

The Ducks

*I*T ALL STARTED WITH SOME CLOTHESLINE. I'M NOT SURE IF Mama and my older sister Gladys really needed it or if they just wanted to get me out of their hair for a few minutes. I confess that I have always suspected the latter.

They were making a dress for Gladys. Scraps of material, patterns, straight pins, and thread were scattered all over the floor. Keenly sensitive from birth, I sensed right off that my running through their little piles was upsetting to them. This wasn't totally unusual. They tended to misconstrue my helpful intentions.

After failing to divert my attention with suggestions that I climb a rope, fly a kite, play in the street, or eat mud pies, they suggested that I go to the "hardwest" store. (I was eighteen when I realized this was supposed to be hard*ware* rather than hard*west*. Somehow hardwest still sounds better to me.) They said they needed rope for a clothesline. Looking back on it, that seems rather illogical. But what the heck did I know? I was only five.

In 1940s Mississippi, it was perfectly reasonable to send a five-year-old to the store. The streets to be crossed were mostly devoid of traffic, and I was known (a gross understatement) to every house along the way. It was a three-block walk from our house up Mitchell Street to North State Street. North State was the major highway through town. However, I didn't have to cross it. I just had to turn left, and the hardwest store would be the third building down.

Giving me twenty-five cents, Mama told me to be careful and by all means to take my time. I kept the money, two dimes and a nickel, tightly pressed in my right hand as I crossed Gunter Street, a gravel road, and headed up Mitchell. When I reached the top of the hill, I looked across the street into Mrs. Clark's yard and saw two large ducks making their way toward me.

Honest to God, I hadn't done a thing to those ducks—certainly nothing to make them cross the street to hunt me down. Later, it was hard to sell that fact, especially to anyone who knew me. But it was true. I swear I didn't do anything to offend them. Until they attacked me, I barely even gave them a thought.

Anyway, here were these huge ducks coming at me, making a horrible racket. As I recall, they were six feet, maybe seven feet tall. I stood frozen as I stared at the monsters. I couldn't move. I couldn't scream. I just stood there paralyzed.

Within seconds, the beasts were on me like stink on a skunk. In moments I was rolling on the ground screaming, crying, kicking, praying, and being pecked unmercifully. Just when all seemed lost, mere seconds before I crossed the abyss to the Pearly Gates, a car stopped on the hill and the driver ran to my rescue. Picking the beasts off of me with a hand around each of their necks, he carried them back across the street and flung them in the general direction of Mrs. Clark's.

By the time the animals hit the ground, I was at least three hundred yards away. I never even thanked my Good Samaritan. As the monster ducks fled, flapping their wings and squawking loudly, I ran as fast as I could to the only place a person can go for refuge and consolation at a time like this. I wanted my Mama. I wanted to leap up into her outstretched arms and bury my head in her bosom.

Instead, she greeted me coolly. "Where's the rope?" she asked.

Could this really be? I had almost had my ears plucked off, and all she was interested in was the rope?

I said nothing, so she asked again. "Where's the rope?"

"Er .... I don't have it."

"Oh, for heaven's sake! I should have known better. Where's the money?"

"Er .... er .... I guess I don't have that either."

"Well, what happened to it?"

"The….er….the….er….ducks….er….the ducks got me!" I said, my hands in my pockets and my head hanging down.

Well, even those loud, squawking ducks had not prepared me for the cackling I was about to hear.

"The ducks got him! The ducks got him! Gladys, come listen to this one! It's the best yet!" Mama called.

Gladys came running. She was such a little goody-goody; she loved it when I was in trouble. "Go ahead, tell Gladys what you just told me," Mama urged.

I stood silent. Clearly her laughter was a bad sign.

"Well, go ahead," she repeated. "Tell her what you just told me."

"The ducks got me," I said shyly, looking down at my feet.

I spent the next few minutes watching two respectable females rolling on the floor in sidesplitting laughter. Best not to pursue the subject, I decided. Maybe if I could just fade quietly away, they would forget all about it. At least they were having so much fun that they didn't seem interested in punishing me. It wasn't much consolation. I never had a spanking that hurt as much as their howls of glee.

My hopes that they would forget the whole incident were doomed to failure. Over time, the story was often repeated. Each time it seemed to bring on louder laughter than before, and each time I got a little quieter. I never once came to my own defense.

A few weeks later Gladys started the fifth grade, and Mama and Daddy decided they needed a set of encyclopedias. A salesman came to the house one night and sat with my parents, discussing what I considered to be a lot of boring stuff. About the third time I interrupted, the salesman looked up. "That's the little boy I got the geese off of!" he exclaimed. "I swear, if I hadn't come along, I do believe they would have killed him!"

I wanted to kiss that man right on the mouth! Revenge was sweet. Mama and Gladys felt so bad that I almost felt sorry for them.

I swear, they were so syrupy and sweet for the next few days I could hardly stand it. I think it lasted until I set the hair of Gladys's favorite doll on fire, but that's another story.

The Drum

DADDY HAD A BEAUTIFUL SNARE DRUM WITH PEARL SIDES, which had been given to him by the Shriners. He loved that drum more than just about anything. He kept it in a black case, and it sat in a special place in his workshop in the garage. I had very strict instructions not to even look at it, let alone touch it. As you will probably have guessed, from most people such admonitions wouldn't have stopped me for long. However, instructions from my father carried a little more weight than from the average dancing bear.

Daddy had taught himself to drum as a boy. The only child of a mother in poor health, he had spent much of his childhood in isolation. He wasn't allowed to make any kind of noise in the house. Nor was he often allowed to leave, as they wanted him close by so they could keep tabs on him. Daddy had access to his father's tools and woodpile. He also found a pair of drumsticks somewhere. He taught himself to build things out of the wood and to play the drum, the latter by copying what he saw the drummers do as the band played the score for silent movies.

Daddy did a good job teaching himself. Much of his later life was spent in different types of woodwork, and he became an incredible drummer. He gave drum lessons when he was twelve years old and started the Shrine Drum Corps in Jackson when he was eighteen. This was quite an accomplishment, especially when you consider he wasn't a Shriner at the time. He was asked to join the Marine Band, an invitation that he truly wanted to accept. Sadly, his parents wouldn't let him. They knew that all musicians were alcoholics who hung around in bad places, smoked cigarettes, kissed girls, and probably said bad words. Many were even thought to have told dirty jokes, but that, of course, was pure speculation. By the time I was born, Daddy had no interest in drumming as a profession, but he still cherished his drum and remained active in the Shrine Drum Corp and the newly organized Shrine Marching Band.

I left the drum untouched until I was about six, when the circus came to town. Daddy took me out of school early that day. It was only time I can ever remember him doing that—in fact, until then I wasn't sure he knew where the school was. Once out of school, we hurried to the fairgrounds to watch the men and elephants put up the gigantic circus tent known as the Big Top. I don't know what the kids left behind were learning in school that day, but I can assure you it wasn't nearly as exciting as what we witnessed that afternoon.

The shirtless, tattooed men stood around in a circle. One by one they pounded iron stakes into the ground with their sledgehammers. If even one man's timing had been slightly off it would have been a great day for the local orthopedist, good for at least six broken wrists. But they never missed; their rhythm was perfect. Their hammers passed each other within fractions of an inch, but they never touched.

We spent the rest of the afternoon observing the wonderful array of strange people and watching the elephants effortlessly attack the enormous tasks of raising the Big Top. The tent started in a pile on the ground, with long ropes coming off from it in all directions. The ropes were attached to the elephants that stood still in a perfect circle surrounding the tent. When a whistle was blown, the elephants started walking, pulling the ropes taut. Slowly, the huge tent rose magically to its full height and the center pole was put in place. The ropes were removed from the elephants and secured to the iron stakes that had already been driven into the ground. It was an astonishing process, and the epitome of teamwork. Everyone, man and beast, knew exactly what he was to do and exactly when he was to do it.

The rest of the afternoon, Daddy and I ate cotton candy, hot dogs, and candy apples. That night we had front-row seats at the circus. Next to the trapeze act and all the animals going poo-poo all over the place, the thing that made the biggest impression on me was the animal tamer. I was amazed to see him crack his whip and push a chair right in the face of the ferocious animals. The best moment was when two beautiful tigers jumped through flaming hoops—hoops that looked a lot like daddy's drum—while roaring and slapping their paws menacingly at him. I knew right then what I wanted to be when I grew up. Admittedly, it wasn't my first career plan, but it was definitely the best. In my mind, I started emulating the animal tamer right then and there.

In the garage the following day, I had my makeshift whip in one hand and my mother's dining room chair in the other. I was fighting and taming the fiercest animals in all of Africa. There were tigers, bears, lions, alligators, several charging rhinoceroses, two dinosaurs, and the neighbor's dog. All cowered back, deathly afraid of my whip and my supremacy.

But wait. I stopped to think. Was this really the life I wanted to pursue? My daddy wasn't an animal tamer, and if there was one thing I was sure of, it was that I had to be just like my daddy.

As I began to return to reality, I spotted the pearl drum in the corner. Perfect! I did not have to deny my father after all. Nor did I have to turn my back on my newfound dreams of applause, daring and life in the wild animals' cage. I could easily combine the two. She might not have liked me, but my Sunday school teacher had been right. Where there's a will, there's a way. There *was* a God!

I carefully placed the drum on its side, the same way the circus hoops had been positioned. I held up my whip, signaling for a drum roll. A hush fell over the crowd. Lowering my head and carefully timing my steps, I ran toward the drum—in my mind's eye, the sides were flaming by now—and leapt through it to thunderous applause. I took off my top hat; an animal tamer's hat never falls off during a death-defying act. I also tried not to notice the way my great leap had shredded my "hoop." Turning my back to the animals, knowing that I now had total control over them, I cracked my whip loudly and bowed deeply to an astonished audience.

It doesn't get any better than this: a hat trick and a grand slam, all in one. Actually, to be perfectly honest, I guess the applause wasn't all that thunderous. In truth, the real thunder started when my father went out into the garage that night and spotted the drum.

Daddy Bogue

"GRANDMOTHER! GRANDMOTHER! C'MERE, QUICK! THERE'S A man at your front door with a suitcase!"

I was at Grandmother Keeton's house drinking the milk shake she had just made for me. Unlike the Big House that my Fondren grandparents lived in, my Keeton grandparents' house was a small bungalow. Set at the back of a deep lot, the little house was supposed to be replaced by a larger home, but the plan never materialized.

Grandmother Keeton was pretty much what was then called a shut-in and would now be called a cardiac cripple. Granddaddy Keeton, a bookkeeper, worked from home so he could take care of her. Though the house was small, it was filled with love and I adored going there. Grandmother and Granddaddy Keeton would sit in the living room with me, telling me stories of their childhoods and my father's boyhood as well. We would play I Spy and Chinese checkers. Grandmother Keeton constantly corrected my grammar. But she was so sweet-natured that when she did so, it seemed like good information rather than criticism.

Grandmother Keeton had made the milkshake by putting a well beaten egg, sugar and vanilla extract in the bottom of a glass, filling the glass with milk, and topping it off with nutmeg. I was truly savoring this delicious concoction when I spotted the intruder on the porch. Naturally, I felt that one of my jobs there was to alert the family to any events of note taking place on or around the property.

"Is he smoking a pipe?" she asked, inquiring about the intruder.

"Yes'm, he sure is," I said.

"Oh dear," she said as she hurried to the door. "Just as I thought, it's Daddy Bogue," she mumbled, not seeming at all pleased.

"Who is Daddy Boat?" I asked from behind her.

"Bogue. Daddy Bogue. He's my father. Your father's grandfather, and your great- grandfather," she said quickly as she hurried to the door. I should note here that I don't think I ever learned where the name "Bogue" came from. Or, if I did, I've forgotten.

"You mean Daddy has a granddaddy too?" It was a new concept for me. I didn't know *anybody* was that old.

Despite his age, Daddy Bogue was a rather nice-looking old man. He had beautiful white hair, a protuberant belly that reminded me of Santa, and a neck that hung way down from his chin. "You must be Billy," he said, smiling, leaning over and placing a dime in my hand. "I'm looking forward to getting to know you."

He seemed to really mean it. For an adult, he sure seemed friendly. I liked him right away.

Grandmother, on the other hand, seemed rather reserved toward this unexpected visitor. "Why didn't you let us know you were coming?" she asked, sounding the way she did when she asked me why I had smeared the jar of strawberry jam all over her kitchen table earlier that morning.

"Just wanted to surprise you."

"I see," Grandmother answered. "How long will you be staying?"

"Few days. Maybe a week."

"I'll just bet," Grandmother said, still sounding exasperated. "You know we barely have enough room for ourselves." That was God's truth. Granddaddy Keeton said that house was so small you had to go outside to cuss the cat.

Since six-year-olds don't know much about either in-laws or the correlation between long visits and stale fish, I never did understand why my grandparents seemed less than excited by Daddy Bogue's presence. It was much later in life that it dawned on me that his airy "few days to a week" turned into several years. In fact, Daddy Bogue took up permanent residence in the back room that had previously functioned as Granddaddy's bookkeeping office, which couldn't have been very convenient for Granddaddy. In the end, Daddy Bogue didn't leave their home until the day he died and was carried out of it.

Daddy Bogue and I became fast friends, with the natural affinity that develops between the very young and the very old. Because the middle-aged are generally too busy to fool with either one of them, both groups are eager to find someone who will really listen. Someone on the opposite end of the age spectrum, who has all the time in the world, doesn't say, "Not right now" or "Tell me later." They say things like, "Tell me more." It doesn't matter to either that one may be mentally woolly while the other can't read or write. These natural allies don't come in contact with each other as much these days, with entire industries now dedicated to taking care of the very old and the very young. To my mind, both lose something from the change.

The time we spent together was wonderful—and Daddy Bogue always had time for me. He would smoke his pipe, blow smoke rings, and do tricks like pulling off his thumb and pulling nickels from my ear. I don't recall ever going anywhere with him. Except for occasionally sitting on the back porch, we never even went outside. We just talked. I would listen to Daddy Bogue tell stories for hours on end, hanging on every word. The fact that I had heard each story many times before never mattered. No matter how many times he told me of being a United States marshal and chasing down bad guys and gunslingers, I was rapt.

This put him in the category of Allen "Rocky" Lane, one of my favorite cowboys of the Saturday afternoon matinees at the Pix Theater.

Daddy Bogue often told me about hanging desperadoes. I assume this happened after they had been duly tried, but we really didn't get into such small details. Just in case I was ever in the same situation, he taught me how to tie a perfect hangman's knot. Later on, in Boy Scouts, I would learn to tie many knots, but two half hitches, the square knot and the hangman's knot are the only ones I remember, and Daddy Bogue had taught me all of them long before the Scouts got to me. I haven't had an occasion to use the hangman's knot just yet, although I have certainly considered it several times.

He taught me a lot of other things as well. I still remember his lessons on knives. He said that the only true test to determine if a knife was sharp was its ability to cut, not tear, paper. He taught me how to sharpen a knife, but also told me never to buy a dull one. "If the man that made it couldn't sharpen it, you can't either," he said.

Daddy Bogue's stories were so colorful that even my six-year-old self wondered at first if they were tall tales. But then he told me about catching snakes by the tail and "popping" them like a whip to break their necks. Afterward, Grandmother described an occasion when a snake had been chasing her, and Daddy Bogue handled the situation in just this manner. That was all I needed; I never doubted his veracity again.

Daddy Bogue may have been shiftless, unreliable, and "full of a lot of hot air," as others said, but I loved that old man. If I ran the universe I would put a Daddy Bogue in every child's life: a kind, cheerful elder with the time and inclination to pass on stories of their family past and the wide world beyond, listen to their own stories and questions, and above all, make them feel important. It's a humbling thought—that it's not so much our achievements that make us special, but the fact that we can make others feel special themselves

The Piano

*E*VEN NOW, SO MANY DECADES LATER, I CAN'T EXPLAIN WHY I did the things I did as a child. It was probably some force in the universe too powerful to be denied. At the time, of course, what I was doing just seemed logical. Like the time I decided to play the piano with my father's drumsticks. As I've said, my father was a terrific drummer, and I idolized him. It only made sense that I wanted to be a drummer also. Daddy always used a drum, but there I parted company with him. Playing a drum seemed rather boring to me, especially when we had a piano sitting around that nobody ever paid any attention to. Little-boy logic told me that it made excellent sense to combine these two percussion instruments.

I had been standing there for a few moments with the drumsticks raised high over my head, contemplating the melodious effect the combination of musical instruments would produce, when my mother appeared from out of nowhere. She always seemed to do that at times like these. Immediately realizing what was about to take place, she yelled, "Billy! So help me, if you so much as touch that piano I am going to wear you out!" Translated, that meant "I'm going to spank the living hell out of you," but, of course, Mama didn't say things like that.

It was a moment of decision. I shot her a quick glance out of the corner of my eye, then a quick look back at the piano keys, so untouched and inviting. Another quick look toward Mama, who was closing in fast. There was fire in her eyes, her hand was raised, and my destiny was certain. Quickly my child's brain weighed the options. There was no doubt she meant what she said. Unlike the parents of some of my friends, she always delivered as promised. One thing about Mama—you could always depend on her! So why go through with it? Why not just say, "Only kidding!" and walk away? That would probably result in a short "talking to," a hug, and maybe even some cookies.

This is where the universal force I mentioned kicked in. Some things are bigger than all of us. Intellectual curiosity must prevail, even in the face of adversity. And in this situation, I felt that the entire world of music awaited the results of the experiment. For all I knew, no one had ever combined drumsticks and piano before. At times like these, one must not be held back by fear of loss of limb, life, of a blistered backside. Such were my thoughts, though I might not have put them in exactly these words at the time.

"I mean it!" my mother shrieked as I took one last quick look at the keys. The "you little bastard" that followed the first three words of this sentence was implied. She would never have said such a thing, not even to herself, despite the fact that it would have been totally justifiable. She probably also recognized the irony of calling her own son a bastard. But I digress.

Destiny called, and I answered. I slammed the drumstick forcefully on the first three piano keys in rapid succession, using every bit of force I could muster. I might have been little, but when I put my mind to it I was pretty strong. I managed to get off two more strikes by the time Mama reached me. One of the five keys lost its ivory, two cracked, and the other two only chipped.

My arm was raised to hit the sixth key. Mama grabbed my wrist with her left hand, spun me around, and threw me over her lap. Dirty Harry

Callahan would have been proud of the move. Pulling the drumstick from my grip, in one fluid motion she laid it across my posterior thighs multiple times in the next few seconds.

She never hit me on my fanny—the portion of my anatomy properly referred to as buttocks by anyone north of Memphis. Firstly, there was too much padding there, and secondly, she wanted to be sure to get below the level of my short pants to insure maximum sting. As I've said before, the fact that Mama pondered such fine points of punishment didn't make her a sadist, or even mean-spirited. Such knowledge of the subtleties of pain were inborn, I think, well known to all Southern women…or at least to all the many females who spanked me on a regular basis.

And so my experiments in percussion ended in ignominy. How can we ever expect to experience new musical frontiers with this kind of oppression? I have to wonder if Beethoven, Bach, Rachmaninoff, or Elvis had to overcome such overwhelming odds. The sound of the drumsticks on the piano keys has long since been forgotten, but I will always remember the sound of those sticks hitting my backside, and it wasn't particularly melodious.

—

Jackie

THERE WERE WIDESPREAD FEELINGS, AMONG MY FAMILY AND Jackson at large, that I was a bad little boy. I believe this assumption was based on a total misrepresentation of the facts. Now, I realize that there was more than a little incriminating evidence, like the fact that I averaged twelve spankings a day until I was six years old, getting nine one morning before breakfast and thirteen one morning before Sunday school. (You have to remember that Sunday school didn't start until almost ten o'clock, so it's not as bad as it might sound.) There was also to the indubitable fact that Mama's spanking arm was a full three inches larger than the other one. All of this misleading evidence notwithstanding, I'll proceed to prove my point.

Which is this: things would have been different if people had realized that I had a playmate named Jackie. The truth of the matter is I was really a pretty good little kid. Jackie, on the other hand, was a terror. He did all sorts of things, really bad things, and laid the blame for all of them on me. I don't know why I stuck with him as long as I did, because he was always getting me into trouble.

I remember one time when the living room lamp was broken. Hearing the noise, Mama came running. When she demanded an explanation,

I explained to her calmly that I had been quietly sitting on the couch minding my own business and reading my Bible like a good little boy when Jackie broke her favorite lamp for no reason whatsoever. Maybe it was that she was naturally suspicious, as all mothers are, or because there was no one else around (Jackie had a way of disappearing at such times), or because she thought I wasn't actually reading Deuteronomy… but for whatever reason, Mama took it out on me.

Incredibly coincidental as it may sound, I pledge you my word that the exact same thing happened when the bedroom window was broken, the garage light was broken, Aunt May's hat got squashed, and a frog turned up in Mama's washing machine. Nowhere to be found every single time, Jackie always left me to bear the brunt of the punishment. It wasn't that I minded all the trips to the Hoorah Patch. God knows I was pretty well used to them. What bothered me more was the way he was impugning my otherwise spotless reputation. (And that brings up another point. I never did know why the Fondrens called a whipping "going to the Hoorah Patch." The only thing I can figure is that it sounds a bit more genteel to say "Little Billy went to the Hoorah Patch last night" rather than "I spanked the daylights out of the little bastard again." I should also mention, in case it's not clear from my many references to it, that the Hoorah Patch wasn't an actual place, located for example back behind our kitchen door. As the next anecdote illustrates, I could be brought to the Hoorah Patch at any moment and in virtually any place.)

As time went on I started getting really fed up with Jackie. Things between us came to a head one day when I started crying for no apparent reason right in the middle of a church service. Daddy picked me up and carried me outside. He didn't seem at all upset. As a matter of fact, he seemed to be glad to be outside—he never was much for preaching anyway. He took off his coat, sat under the tree, leaned back and lit up a Chesterfield. He took a long, slow drag, and as the smoke began to escape from his nose he asked, "Why did you start crying anyway?"

"Jackie pinched me," I replied. Well, just the mention of Jackie's name made him mad. There he was, sitting outdoors enjoying life just as big as you please. Then as soon as I mentioned Jackie's name, Daddy jumped up and carried me to the Hoorah Patch, right in front of God and everybody leaving the church. As I explained in an earlier chapter, Daddy didn't carry me to the Hoorah Patch very often—he usually let Mama have that job. But you can believe me when I tell you, when he did it was quite a memorable trip.

As this suggests, by that point Jackie was getting me into an awful lot of trouble. So when Aunt Mary suggested on the way home from the movie one night that it was time for me to get rid of him, it seemed like the thing to do. I simply picked him up, threw him down the storm drain, and that was that. I neither saw nor heard from him again. Later in life, I attempted the same approach when it seemed desirable to end certain other relationships. But it never seemed to work as well with them as it had with Jackie. Apparently, imaginary people are just easier to get rid of than real ones.

I never thought I'd say this, but I really miss Jackie. He was agreeable, he always let me have my way, and he never asked to share my Tootsie Rolls. He was also a genius at finding creative ways to cut the boredom out of everyday life. With Jackie around, no day was ordinary. If he had just taken his share of the trips to the Hoorah Patch, we'd probably still be friends today.

Paint, 2

A S YOU ALREADY KNOW, WHEN I WAS A CHILD I HAD A STRONG affinity for paint. Undeterred by my unfortunate encounter with Mr. Harrison, the house painter, I heard paint's siren call again one day when I was making my way home from the Fondren Grocery to our home at 304 Mitchell Street. I passed by the Magees' house on Oxford Street only to see Mr. Magee was painting the front door dark gray—the color that would later be called charcoal, at least outside of Mississippi. He was about halfway done when I heard Mrs. Magee calling him to come in to supper.

He left the paintbrush neatly on top of the can and went inside to eat. I may have been only five or six years old, but I knew at once that I should look this situation over carefully. Intent on making sure that Mr. Magee's work was up to neighborhood standards, I climbed the three steps to the small wooden porch of the bungalow. Looking closely at the portion of the door that was newly painted, I was instantly pleased with the quality of his work. There was no problem at all and probably nothing that I could do to help, as Mr. Magee seemed to have every-thing under satisfactory control. I could therefore proceed on home to my favorite supper of baked sweet potatoes, turnip greens, black-eyed peas, and peach cobbler.

As I was preparing to leave, however (if there wasn't a "however," this would be a rather pointless story), I noticed something odd. While the door looked very nice, Mr. Magee had done absolutely nothing about the floor of the porch. It should have been obvious to anyone that the green floor of the porch did not match the front door. Of course, Mr. Magee wasn't a professional painter. He therefore lacked the keen eye for color, coordination, flair, and style that only a few of us were fortunate to receive. This being the case, I benevolently decided to lend a helping hand.

I quickly picked up the brush and began to paint one corner of the porch. The improvement was readily obvious. I especially liked the effect that my tennis shoes made as they tracked paint on the rest of the floor. (This was before the days such shoes were called "sneakers.") Having left a gentle hint of what needed to be done and not wanting to steal from Mr. Magee the satisfaction of a task well completed, I left without seeking praise or reward. There's just nothing like helping a neighbor to make a guy feel good.

Soon after I arrived home, I told my mother what I had done. As usual, she failed to appreciate my artistic efforts. I bet Leonardo and Pablo would have ended up as fishermen, plumbers, or automobile mechanics if they had had to put up with this kind of misunderstanding and abuse. Rewarding me with her usual love taps, she instructed me to call Mrs. Magee. When I asked why, Mama said I needed to ask Mrs. Magee if she wanted to spank me as well. As I trembled, Mama dialed the number and told Mrs. Magee that I wanted to speak to her. Then she thrust the phone at me, saying, "Go ahead!"

Sheepishly, I took the phone. "Er… er… mmmmm, Mama says, er… er… do you… I mean, er… do you want her to… er, bring me, er… to your h-h-h-h-house so you can er… you know, er… s-s-s-s-spank me too?" I asked in a trembling voice. Mrs. Magee immediately replied that she thought this an absolutely wonderful idea and that she would wait outside for us.

This conversation with Mrs. Magee was the first time I can ever remember talking on the phone. Not having any previous experience with telecommunications, I failed to understand that my mother could not hear what Mrs. Magee had just said. When Mama demanded to know what her response was, I should have replied, "Mrs. Magee said that though she was grateful for the offer, an extra spanking would be quite unnecessary, as she feels certain that your darling little boy has learned a valuable lesson from this unfortunate occurrence. And she said to be sure to tell you that sweet Little Billy could drop by for milk and cookies any time he is in the neighborhood, as she always loves to see the little dear."

But, thinking that Mama actually knew what that witch—I mean, what Mrs. Magee—had said, I simply replied, "I th... th... I think she was ju... ju... just k-k-kidding." Whereupon I was immediately escorted to the Magees' house, not just by Mama but by both of my parents together. It is no wonder that I hate telephones to this day.

I suspect that few men have ever walked to the gallows with more trepidation or sense of humiliation than I felt walking to the Magees' that evening. No punishment that Mrs. Magee could have dealt out could have been nearly as bad as the anticipation of what lay ahead.

Though Mrs. Magee had been quite upset when I talked to her on the phone (some people get mad at the darnedest little things), by the time we got to her house she had cooled off a bit. She still looked quite stern and determined, but when I marched straight up to her and announced that I was there for my spanking, she seemed to sort of melt. I suspect that she may have also been a bit hesitant to raise a hand toward me with my father watching her. Daddy could certainly be intimidating, and it was nice to have that working in my favor for a change.

That said, he had a lesson to deliver as well. A genuine woodworking craftsman, as I have already described, my father was very meticulous with paint. He always put professional finishes on everything he made. He used a spray gun to put on ten to twelve coats of paint or varnish, sanding between coats and insisting that each be without a single blemish. The results were magnificent. But while he enjoyed painting with a spray gun, I have never known anyone to hate painting with a brush as much as Daddy did.

To make things right with the Magees, Daddy had to repaint the floor of the porch. Being so meticulous, he also not only finished the door that Mr. Magee had started, but also painted the screen door and the little window that opened onto the porch, both of which Mr. Magee probably had no intention of painting in the first place. Naturally, all of this had to be done by brush. By the time it was over, I think Daddy felt lucky that the Magees did not require him to paint their entire house to make up for his son's moment of creativity.

Having to straighten up my mess was burdensome for Daddy, and therefore for me. Somehow, during the process, he convinced me to abandon my aspirations of painting as my life's work. I'm not sure just exactly how he did this. Possibly it was his gentle parental encouragement toward an exciting and rewarding future as a septic tank maintenance man. Or possibly it was the threat of the loss of both thumbs and the use of my left foot. I don't remember exactly, I just know that by the end I had given up my future as a house painter. It's a shame, really. I was so darn good at it.

Uncle Snooks

*O*N A BEAUTIFUL SPRING DAY IN MISSISSIPPI, EVERYONE SEEMED to be working outside: cleaning out flower beds, clearing gutters, painting porch furniture, walking around making plans for future projects, or composing "honey-do" lists for some unwary spouse.

Uncle Snooks, Granddaddy Frondren's only living son, was no exception. By way of background, I should note that Granddaddy Fondren did a lot of things very well. He was a successful businessman, postmaster, church deacon, real estate speculator, and father of eight. In the paternal vein he was very good at producing girl children, with seven to his credit. But he wasn't good at producing boys, fathering one who lived for less than a year and David Fulton Fondren Jr. You would think that as the only boy in the family, David Jr. deserved to be called by a boyish name, but Snooks was pretty much all I ever heard him called, for reasons I never discovered.

At age six, I had no particular place to go that beautiful spring morning when I left Fondren Grocery and began my lazy walk toward home. Along the way, I spotted a portion of brick at the edge of the walk. As you may already have realized, noticing things on walks around the neighborhood tended to get me into trouble.

At that time, all of us in Jackson referred to bricks as "brickbats." The one I spotted was less than a quarter of a brickbat, maybe an eighth of a whole brick. It was irregular and had jagged edges. I kicked it over to the center of the sidewalk and then kicked it again with each few steps as I ambled my way along.

As I meandered, I greeted the many people working outdoors. All quickly encouraged me to move on to a destination somewhere farther along than their property. So I continued kicking the brick down North State Street and turned left on Fondren Place. There wasn't a sidewalk on Fondren Place, but there was a curb on the side of the street, and the brick would bounce off the curb back toward the center of the street as I made my way up the small hill.

Uncle Snooks's house was at the corner of North State and Fondren Place. On my way up the hill, I spied him standing on a ladder in front of a window on the side of his house. The ladder was straddling a rather large and thorny rose bush. Painting this window must have been a spur-of-the-moment decision because Uncle Snooks wasn't wearing the old clothes you would expect to see on someone involved in a painting project. Instead, he was wearing a white shirt, tie, slacks, and dress shoes. Perhaps he was a sudden and unwary victim of one of the honey-do lists I have mentioned.

Uncle Snooks was standing on the next-to-the-top step of the ladder, holding a four-inch-wide paintbrush. On the shelf on the opposite side of the ladder was a bucket of dark green paint. If the fact that I spied a brickbat had not already warned you that this tale wouldn't end well, the mention of paint should surely do it.

Still unaware of me, Uncle Snooks bent over, dipped the brush in the bucket, and wiped the excess paint off it, first on one side of the bucket and then the other. He then applied the brush to the top edge of the window frame, being very careful not to get the dark green paint on the windowpane. His house sat on a lot with a small side yard, and the curb was about fifteen feet from the side of the house. While I stood there and watched him paint diligently away, I noticed the piece of brick, still lying next to the curb. I picked up the brick and, as I held it in my hand, decided it would be fun to toss the piece of brickbat into Uncle Snooks's paint can.

Obviously, there were numerous problems with this idea. If the brick missed the bucket, it could easily break the window—not a good idea. It could hit Uncle Snooks—a downright bad idea. It could have caused him to fall off the ladder into the rose bush—an even worse idea. Or it could have caused him to fall into the glass window—a really, *really* bad idea. I actually made very detailed calculations about all this, having mastered calculus by the age of three while reading Deuteronomy, but I will not bore you with those details.

But none of that stopped me. Instead, I just reasoned that if I was going to go through with an idea with so many dreaded possibilities, I absolutely had to get a good feel for the weight of the brick, so that I could accurately calculate the proper distance and arc necessary to have it land in the middle of the bucket.

I would very much like to be able to tell you that, after making all of these calculations and carefully weighing the risks and possible rewards of the toss, I decided not even to try such a foolish idea. That I greeted my uncle and offered to help him with his project in any way that I could. That after I helped him, he invited me in for a nice cup of tea while we reread the morning devotional.

Unfortunately, I never gave that idea a split second's consideration. What was to consider? I wanted to throw the brickbat into the middle of Uncle Snooks' paint can. I never once considered that it might go anywhere other than exactly where I intended for it to go. I wasn't even careful when I tossed it. I just gave it a throw.

And it went right into the center of the can.

At which point I realized that the calculations I should have been concerned with had to do with Uncle Snooks's reaction to the dark green paint that immediately splattered onto the window, the white house and Uncle Snooks himself, dress clothes and all. I also should have calculated an escape route. Instead, I was so stunned at the results of my toss that I forgot to run. I did enter the house with Uncle Snooks after all, but it was at his order rather than invitation, and there was no mention of tea or devotionals.

Uncle Bob

*M*AMA HAD SIX SISTERS AND ONE BROTHER. ALL OF MY aunts except Aunt May married, so I ended up with a bunch of uncles. I am certain that each and every one of these would like to have wrung my neck much of the time, but they were all wonderful gentlemen. I can't remember any of them ever saying a cross word to me, although they all teased me constantly.

I had Sunday dinner with all them every week at the Big House. All of them were fun, and all of them, in one way or another, were role models for me.

This was especially true of Uncle Bob. Aunt Margaret was married to Bob Striger, an engineer who studied math his entire life. While he may have been considered a mite eccentric by the rest of the group, he always had a big smile on his face and at least four pair of dime-store glasses in his shirt pocket. He would often wear two and sometimes three pair at once. He said he could never understand why anyone would go to the eye doctor for endless questions about which combination of lenses was best when he could go the dime store and do the same thing for less than a dollar.

He also usually had several cigars in his shirt pocket, although I never knew him to smoke. Rather, he would either stick a cigar in his mouth and chew on the end of it, or he would bite off the end and chew on that. Another thing I remember about him was that he always wore white socks. This was before the '50s, when all the kids wore white socks. I think one of the reasons I remember this so well was because when I was eight years old I received a shoe shine kit for Christmas. I proudly went around shining all of my uncles' shoes for a dime a pair. This was going pretty well until I brought my kit to Uncle Bob. Somehow I got black shoe polish all over his white socks. I felt terrible, but he never said a word. He just smiled and acted like he didn't even notice.

I had great difficulty learning to tell time. Mama worked tirelessly with me on this. Daddy would draw circle after circle on sheets of paper and put in all the numbers. Both tried multiple different approaches, but the idea of it just wouldn't sink into my thick skull.

One Sunday morning, I was sick enough to be excused from Sunday school and church. I guess everyone must have thought I was terminal because I can't imagine being excused otherwise. We were talking about my problems with telling time. Uncle Bob, who later became a pillar of the local Presbyterian Church but at that time never darkened the church's doors, said he would teach me.

Aunt May immediately took me off to the side. Uncle Bob was a very smart man, she warned me. Way too smart for me to understand. "If you let him try to teach you to tell time," she said, "he will have you so confused, you may never learn. So just tell him, 'No, thank you.'"

Soon thereafter, everyone but Uncle Bob and I left for church. He was sitting in a chair, reading the Sunday paper, while I was playing on the floor. "Billy, do you want me to teach you to tell time? It's really not hard at all," he asked with his usual warm smile.

"Yes, sir," I answered, jumping up in his lap.

He took off his wristwatch and began to demonstrate. First, he explained, you looked at the big hand to see if it was on the "before" side or the "after" side of the clock. If it was on the "after" side, you counted down to see how many minutes "after" it was. Then you looked at the short hand to see which number it had just passed. If the long hand was on the "before" side, you would count up to see how many minutes "before" it was, then you looked at the short hand to see the next number it would reach. Then he showed me how the hands looked to show the "o'clock" and the "thirty" readings, and we were done!

"Gosh, is this all there is to it? This is *easy*," I exclaimed as I hugged his neck.

When the family returned from church a little over an hour later, I proudly announced that while they were gone, my Uncle Bob had taught me to tell time. Of course, they all knew this was impossible. One after the other began to twist the clock around to different settings, quizzing me extensively along the way. I did not miss a single one.

Uncle Bob taught me three important things that day. The first, obviously, was to tell time. The second was that even well-meaning advice, like the warning offered by Aunt May that Sunday, wasn't always reliable.

Last but not least, the third was that even the most complex and difficult concepts can be mastered easily when they are broken down into bite-sized pieces.

Thanks, Uncle Bob. That was a great life lesson to learn at a very early age. I'm grateful to this day for it, and I'm still sorry that I shined your white socks black.

The Fondren Grocery Store

*G*RANDDADDY'S GROCERY STORE WAS A GATHERING PLACE. IT wasn't only where you purchased your daily bread, it was where you learned the daily news and gossip. You have to remember, this was before television. There wasn't any PBS or CNN. If you wanted to know what was going on in the world, or who was doing what to whom, you could go to Fondren Grocery Store and find out.

In addition to its well-stocked supply of gossip, the store had a lot of advantages that are not available today at any price. For instance, you could call and order your groceries over the phone. Your call might be picked up by Granddaddy, Aunt May, Aunt Ella, or Tisdell. Tisdell was his last name, but as nobody ever called him anything else, I have no idea what his first name was. Tisdell was more or less an assistant manager. In addition to its other staff, the store had a very colorful butcher whose name I can't remember. His arm was emblazoned with a tattoo of a banner with "Mother" written inside of it. Thinking it was a wonderful tribute to his mother, I told him that when I was old enough, I was going to get one just like it. He answered that if I ever even thought about doing such a dumb thing he would snatch my arm off. I never once considered that possibility again, and remain tattoo-free to this day.

Whoever it belonged to, the voice on the other end was interested not only in taking your order but was interested in you as well. After you said you needed milk and bread, the voice on the other end would probably ask if you had enough eggs to get you through the weekend and if your uncle Ned had sobered up from the other night. Then, when asked how the tomatoes were, the voice would probably reply something like "Ripe and beautiful. And by the way, how's little Johnnie Mae doing with the whooping cough?"

Once your order was completed, it was totaled and a carbon copy was placed on the board with all your previous orders so that you could be billed at the end of the month. The original was then given to a clerk, probably Bobby Mayes or Flowers Bacon, high-school kids who worked in the store. They would go through the store placing all your items in a wire basket. The basket would then be placed in the delivery truck and taken to your home.

Most deliveries were made by Floyd, who let me ride with him in the delivery truck sometimes. He was full of colorful comments, and I liked being with him. Upon arriving, he would simultaneously give a quick knock on your door and open it right up. Nobody in Mississippi locked their doors back then. Most people hadn't seen their keys in years. Calling out, "Groceries," he would go straight to the kitchen, where he would put the canned goods and the like on the table and the perishables in the refrigerator. Most people never saw the delivery man. If they did, pleasantries such as, "Is it hot enough for you?" or "How's your mama 'n' 'em?" would be exchanged. (In case you're confused, the latter query is Mississippi for "How are your mother and the rest of your family?") The thought of a tip never entered anyone's mind that I can remember. Not that the service wasn't appreciated. Extra payment just wasn't necessary when the delivery boy was merely doing what he was paid to do.

All of life in those parts came through the Fondren Grocery Store— the rich, the poor; the beautiful and the ugly; the nice and the not-so-nice; the upper crust and the crusty. In part for that reason, I learned a lot about life from that store. In fact, it is somewhat surprising that the folks at a grocery store had so much time to devote to my education. You would think they would be mostly focused on selling or buying, but they always seemed ready to impart a lesson or two as well.

One such lesson—to consider the source of advice before you take it—occurred when I was quite young. A bumblebee had stung me on my left thumb, but all of my relatives were too busy to give me the attention I so richly deserved. Instead, I just crouched down behind the counter of the store and cried. One old-timer who always seemed to be hanging around the store, however, was ready to help. He explained that if I were to pick up a piece of the chewing tobacco stored under the counter and chew it for a while, I would pretty soon forget about my injury.

I did just as he suggested, as he was the only one around who seemed to be the least bit concerned about my welfare. It was great therapy. It was, in fact, one of the few times in my life that a therapy delivered precisely the promised results. The old man was exactly right. In no time at all, I had totally forgotten about the sting. I had even forgotten I had a thumb. I was so busy trying to throw up my toenails that it was at least two days before I remembered anything other than my stomach.

My grandfather died of a heart attack when I was around five. Though his passing must have changed the store in some ways, I wasn't aware of them. Aunt May took over without missing a beat.

The only change I can remember had to do with beer. Beer was never sold in the store, but on Sunday afternoons at the Big House I remember Granddaddy, Daddy, and the other men standing around the kitchen drinking a beer. Of course, this happened after the women folk had cleaned the kitchen and put the Sunday china away, and I don't think anyone had more than one beer.

Aunt May idolized Granddaddy, but she did not share his enthusiasm for the occasional beer. One day after Granddaddy's death a nice gentleman came into the store with some Schlitz advertising signs and a case of Schlitz beer. I overheard him telling Tisdell that he wanted to introduce Schlitz to the store. Tisdell told the man he would have to talk to Aunt May, who was in the office. The salesman tucked some of his signs under his arm as he followed Tisdell to the back of the store. Tisdell winked at me as he walked, and I could see that it was all he could do not to laugh out loud. I couldn't figure out what was so funny until a minute later, when I saw the man running for his life with Aunt May on his heels. Swinging a broom handle at him, she was yelling "Don't you *ever* come in here again!" The salesman forgot to pick up the case of beer when he departed. Being true southern gentlemen who wouldn't want Aunt May further upset, Tisdell, Floyd, and Bobby must have disposed of it.

Aunt May was a stickler for the belief that you had to be nice to all customers, no matter how odd or ornery. One day I got into an argument with a lady I did not know. I can't remember what the dispute was about. I only know that she was being very rude, I knew I was right, and Aunt May even later agreed with me. At the time, though, she intervened immediately, apologizing to the lady for my rude behavior. I was full of righteous indignation. How dare my aunt not take my side? Despite this lesson it took a long time for the philosophy of "The customer is always right" to sink in. Now that I am a customer myself, I frequently find myself wishing that the clerks waiting on me had trained under my Aunt May.

The store also taught me that if someone was paying me to work, I was supposed to *work*, whether there was actually anything to do or not. I was never to stand around, and *never*, under any circumstances, to chat on the telephone. I say "under any circumstances." Perhaps my mother being axed or my dog going mad and attacking the preacher's wife would have been the exceptions, though Aunt May might have disagreed.

There were those, like my Sunday school teacher, who would argue that I never learned anything quickly. But I did learn quickly that if I wasn't busy at the store, I had best find something to do. Otherwise, Aunt May would find something for me to do, and it wouldn't be something I liked.

Have you ever spent time dusting stacks of cans on a grocery store shelf? Shucking the loose outer skins off the onions in a huge vegetable bin? Cleaning the grime from behind a commercial refrigerator? Believe me, it was a lot easier to just pick up a broom and start sweeping an already clean floor, or polish the glass on the already spotless front door. At least then I could drink my Coke while I worked. Once Aunt May set me to a task, I was barely allowed to pause while I was at it, let alone do anything as enjoyable as swigging on my favorite drink.

You may be surprised to hear that it was in the store that I learned about sex, though you won't be surprised to know that it ended up getting me in trouble. I had taken my friend Pat to the back of the store. There, I demonstrated that if we climbed on top of the freezer we could look out through the latticework that went up to the ceiling and "spy" on the people in the store. It was there that Pat chose to tell me about sex. I was fascinated. *Gee whiz,* I thought. Did he really think people actually did that sort of thing?

"If your mama hadn't done it, you wouldn't be here," Pat concluded.

Well, that was going too far. "Now, wait just a minute," I said. "*Your* mama may do it, but mine sure as heck wouldn't!"

"Sure as I'm standing here, she did. If she didn't, you wouldn't have been born," he insisted stubbornly.

I didn't plan it, even for a second. But somehow, my fist landed solidly on his nose. Pat fell backwards off the freezer and landed on the floor, crying bloody murder. His mother and my aunt came running up together to see "my poor little friend" lying there, his nose spewing blood like Old Faithful.

Of course, I was still standing on top of the freezer, no doubt looking like a combination of King Kong and the cat that just ate the canary. Since I couldn't tell these fine Christian ladies why I had decided to use my friend's face for a punching bag—and possibly also because this sort of behavior wasn't entirely uncharacteristic on my part—I made a painfully memorable trip to the Hoorah Patch that day. I'll bet if I had told Aunt May what he had said about my mama, Pat would have gotten the licking instead of me, but of course I couldn't do that. I still wasn't sure it was true. And even if it was, Aunt May, who wasn't married, might not have known about it.

As I grew older, I would work in the store on Saturday mornings from eight until eleven forty-five. I received fifty cents for my labors, not an inconsiderable sum at the time. With my salary in my hand I would rush home, where Mama would give me my fifty cents allowance. Finally, I would run to deposit this vast sum in my savings account before the bank closed at noon. The timing of it all was orchestrated to ensure that I didn't have a single minute to stop and blow my money along the way. This was intended to teach me to be thrifty and provident, but I am not sure that those lessons every really took.

Despite that, I did learn a lot at the store. In addition, finally, to grasping the realities of sex and the philosophy of "The customer is always right," I learned the value of a good work ethic and the importance of being nice to everyone—even if they were being rude to me, offering crazy advice, or telling me things about my mother I didn't want to know. I think I'm a better person for having spent a good portion of my youth at Fondren Grocery Store, and I'm sure my Aunt May would agree.

The N-Word

MOST OF THE STORIES THAT I HAVE TOLD IN THESE WRITINGS have been told, by others and by me, many times over. This particular story has not. I had several decades under my belt before I shared this tale with anyone. Yet there have not been many days when it does not come into my mind.

This book is not the place, and I am not the writer, to try and explain racial attitudes in the Mississippi of the 1940s. The most helpful comment I can make by way of preface is to say that white Southerners of that time had complex and contradictory attitudes toward race. I never saw anyone in my family mistreat a black person; Lee, Liza, and the other black people around us were regarded with love and respect. Yet it was certainly obvious that there was an unspoken difference between them and us, and that we had the upper hand. Similarly, the word "nigger" was often used in Jackson as though it was an ordinary rather than a derogatory word. Yet it was also obvious, if unstated, that this wasn't the proper way to speak of or to black people. I knew this when I was a boy, though I didn't exactly know why.

I didn't think much about any of this until I was seven or so. I was walking on the sidewalk when I noticed a black man coming toward me. As we met I said, "Hi, Nigger." Readers of this book already know I was often "feeling my oats" and looking for excitement. I threw the word out the same way I began many of the other scrapes in this book, with only the vaguest notion of what I was doing, why I was doing it, or what would happen as a result.

I can't imagine what the man was thinking. He said nothing, just lowered his head, looked away from me, and walked calmly by. I think I remember having a wicked little smile on my face.

A short time later I was walking along and met a young black boy roughly my age. Again I said, "Hi, Nigger." And again I noted being met with a lowered head and diverted eyes, but no answer.

The next time I tried this I was walking toward my grandfather's grocery store and met a sweet-looking little old black lady. Again, "Hi, Nigger" was my greeting.

At first, this lady too lowered her head and looked away. Then, however, things changed. "Young man!" I heard her call out after she had walked about five steps past me. I knew immediately that I was in way over my head. Getting into trouble was something with which I was very familiar, but this was something new.

"Ma'am?" I said, trembling as I slowly turned around. This in itself was an arresting response. The children in my family were taught to say "Sir" and "Ma'am" to most people who looked to be older than twelve, but we usually didn't address black people that way.

"Come here!" she said. I slowly stepped toward her. With a stern look on her face and pointing a finger at my nose, asked, "Did you go to Sunday school yesterday?"

"Yes, ma'am."

"Did you go to school today?"

"Yes, ma'am," I whimpered.

Pointing her finger at me again, she asked, "Is that what they taught you in Sunday school yesterday and in school today?"

"No, ma'am," I replied.

"Then why did you say that?"

Of course, I had no answer for her. Now it was *my* head that was lowered, *my* eyes that looked away. They were filled with tears.

As someone who tested every imposed boundary while growing up, I was constantly called down and put in my place. But never, before or since, have I been more ashamed. This lady was a complete stranger, whom I had insulted for no reason whatsoever. Even worse, I had insulted her—assaulted her, in a sense—with a word I did not even really understand, except to know that it was wrong.

One of the things that strikes me now is how brave she was. For all she knew, my father or grandfather could have been a Klansman. They weren't—I didn't know anyone involved with that organization—but she didn't know that. All she knew was that I needed to be straightened out, and that she was going to do it no matter what the consequences.

I've wished for the opportunity to apologize to her, and to tell her what an impact she had on my life. I never knew who she was, and never even saw her again. The same is true of the black man and boy I insulted. Yet I have never forgotten them, and still think of her, in particular, often.

After reading this story, Marty Ward, a good friend and business coach, pointed out that my encounter with this lady, which lasted only a couple of minutes, made a much more lasting and memorable impression than all of my spankings put together.

Marty was correct. I think the reason our encounter was so powerful had to do, at least in part, with the woman's manner. She behaved with a dignity that showed up just how undignified, nasty and disrespectful my own behavior had been. She used a minimum of words and explanation. She not only had the courage to confront me, she had the composure and self-respect to do it without hurling any epithets in return.

In that encounter, regardless of skin color, one of us was clearly a far better human being than the other.

And we both knew who it was.

The Stove

As A BOY, I WAS DEEPLY ENAMORED WITH THE ALL THE WESTERN heroes I saw at the movie theater every Saturday afternoon. I especially loved to emulate my heroes in fierce gunfights. The bad guys would be shooting at me, forcing me to duck behind trees, fence posts or buildings. Bullets would be flying by, just missing me but splintering off pieces of whatever hiding place I was using at the moment. From the angle of the incoming bullets, I always knew exactly where the shots were coming from. I would leap bravely out from behind my shelter and discharge several shots toward my adversaries, either killing them or terrifying them so much with my superior skills as a gunslinger that they scattered like scared rabbits.

Until I was eight, these gunfights were all wholly imaginary. There was nothing I wanted more than a BB gun, but I had been told in no uncertain terms that I couldn't have one until at least my forty-first birthday, if then.

That all changed when I spent several days running a fever and feeling lousy and Mama brought me in to the doctor. I was lying on the examining table at the pediatrician's office when it suddenly occurred to me that Mama and Dr. Burroughs were talking awfully quietly in the corner of the room. I had been paying very little attention to them until their whispering alerted me. Suddenly becoming very interested in their conversation, I heard Dr. Burroughs say, "I'll be with him the whole time, and I will be the one giving him the ether."

As I looked around the room, I couldn't find another *him* there. "Mama, are y'all talking 'bout me? What's ether?" I asked.

"Ssshhh. We'll talk about it later," she said.

Whenever Mama said, "We will talk about it later," "it" was always something I did not want to talk about, later or ever. And while I didn't know what ether was, I didn't want to get it, even with Dr. Burroughs giving it to me. I was already sick, but the thought of "it" and this mysterious ether stuff were making me feel even sicker by now. Mama and the doctor continued to whisper in the corner of the room for what seemed like a long time, but since they now had their backs to me I could no longer hear them.

Once we returned home and Mama put me in the bed, I immediately went to sleep despite my anxiety. When I awakened, Mama and Daddy were standing by the bed. After just looking at me for a while, they said there was something we needed to talk about. Uh-oh. In my experience, "There's something we needed to talk about" was even more ominous than "We'll talk about it later."

Daddy told me that my tonsils were making me sick and that they needed to be removed. There was really nothing to it, he explained. They would take me down to the Baptist Hospital, Dr. Burroughs would put me to sleep, and when I woke up my tonsils would be gone and everything would be fine. But despite his casual tone I could tell right off there was more to it than that, especially since Daddy just stood there rattling the change in his pocket and looking at the ground.

So you'd better believe I answered back fast. I don't remember the exact words, but the gist of them was simple. I did not exactly know what or where my tonsils were; I was, nonetheless, very attached to them. I did not want to part with them, and I certainly did not want

Dr. Burroughs to put me to sleep. My friend Tommy's sick puppy had been put to sleep. After that, he had been wedged into a shoe box, put it in a hole in the ground, and covered up with dirt.

I did not want that to happen to me. "Please don't do me like Tommy's puppy. I promise I'll be *real* good, forever," I begged. "Honest, I won't *ever* do anything bad again. Well, almost never. I promise."

"No, no," Daddy said hastily. "It will be fine, I promise. I had my tonsils out when I was about your age and I did fine. I bet a lot of your friends have already had their tonsils removed, and they did fine too." Clearly guessing that I wasn't buying his sales pitch, he added, "I tell you what I'll do. If you behave and don't give anybody any trouble while this is done, I'll get you that BB gun you've been wanting."

Two sets of eyes, my own and Mama's, popped wide open at that. We both became very excited, though for entirely different reasons.

Holy Toledo! Since I wasn't even sure what my tonsils were, I decided that maybe exchanging them for the coveted BB gun might not be such a bad deal after all. This ether stuff couldn't be worse than Milk of Magnesia or enemas, after all, and I had survived both.

After I agreed to his proposal, Daddy and I were both relieved. We were grinning from ear to ear, but it was obvious that Mama did not share our enthusiasm. "Do you not remember all the trouble he got into with the slingshot you gave him last year?" she said to him.

"That's different," Daddy answered. "I think that little girl was aggravating him, and I don't think he meant to hit the preacher's car. Besides, he's older now. I'll teach him how to shoot it. He'll be fine."

"Well, I just wish we had discussed it first," Mama grumbled. But she knew that once Daddy had made a promise, there would be no backing down.

From that point on, I was so focused on getting the BB gun that the operation flew pretty much out of my mind. I must say, however, that ether stuff was *awful*. It made even an enema, one of that era's great cures for everything from earaches to a bad disposition, seem like a day at the circus. But it didn't matter, because Daddy kept his promise.

When I got home from the hospital, a Daisy Red Ryder BB gun was right there waiting for me. It was love at first sight. The BB gun became my constant companion. I even tried to sneak it into Sunday school. As usual, however, my persnickety Sunday school teacher—as I've noted before, one of the banes of my existence at this time—put her foot down.

Naturally, I used my beloved gun everywhere I could. I shot trees, the foundation of the house, the old chicken coop in back yard, and even the garage. None of these shots left any noticeable marks, and since no window panes were broken, I didn't get into any appreciable trouble.

But one day it was raining and I couldn't go outside. Playing on the small screened porch off of the kitchen, I shot the frame of the screen door and the lattice holding the screen in place. It was then that I noticed a mean-looking *hombre* in the kitchen. As I recall, he was calling me names and saying that my sisters wore combat boots and chewed tobacco. Snarling that he was going to kill me, he reached to draw his six-shooter.

What was a boy to do? Fortunately, the BB gun was cocked and loaded. I was able to shoot him three times before he finished drawing his gun. Unfortunately, I failed to realize my weapon's vast power. I did not know that the same shots that killed an imaginary desperado would go right through him and hit my mother's new stove.

The sound of the BBs hitting the stove was exactly like the bullets ricocheting off of the rocks in the cowboy movies, and that made me happy. My happiness fled a millisecond or so later when I noticed that the shots had not only made small dents in the white porcelain enamel of the stove, but also caused chips about the size of a fifty-cent piece to fly right off it. Mama's beautiful new stove, of which she was so proud, was ruined. Even I could see that.

I might not have understood ether or BBs, but I knew that these were hard times for my family, and that things like stoves did not come easy. I felt horribly ashamed that I had let my parents down in such a big way. There was nowhere to hide and no one I could call on to help. All of a sudden, being in that hole in the ground with Tommy's puppy didn't seem like such a bad place to be.

I don't remember being punished for this heinous crime. Maybe I have repressed that experience. Or maybe my parents didn't punish me. They might have been too busy figuring out whether they should invest in a good psychiatrist, lock me up in a home for the hopelessly deranged, or drop me off at the Methodist orphanage, which was known to take in unloved waifs. I do remember, however, that I did considerably less BB shooting after that, and none of it indoors. It seemed like all of the desperados had vamoosed into other parts, and not a minute too soon.

Evelyn

*S*INCE MY GRANDFATHER AND GRANDMOTHER HAD EIGHT children that lived to adulthood, I had at least a gazillion cousins when I was growing up. As I've said, ours was a huge and close family. The usual head count for our weekly Sunday dinners was around twenty-five or so, counting visitors, children, and whoever was passing by.

As close as we all were, for some strange reason we had very little association with my cousin Evelyn's branch of the of the Fondren family. Evelyn and I were third cousins—our grandfathers were brothers. We were "kissing cousins," as they said, but as I recall we did not do a lot of kissing.

I don't ever remember hearing anything derogatory about any of them, so I have no idea why our families weren't close. Usually, when Mississippi families distance themselves from each other, it can be traced back to hard feelings about a girl, a poker game, or who really won the latest tobacco spitting contest. I don't think any of those contentious issues divided us; our families just didn't get together much.

Despite this, Evelyn and I got to be pretty good buddies, striking up a friendship at school rather than at any family picnic. (Coming from a large family, it wasn't at all unusual to find out someone I knew was actually related to me. Many times in my life I would meet someone and only to learn that we were "kin to once another," or "one another" as folks north of Tupelo might put it. This proved that folks didn't have to look alike or be named alike to be related. (One of my uncles said he thought that Billy the Kid and Jack the Ripper were our cousins, for example, and I had no reason not to believe him.)

But Evelyn and I somehow became fascinated with the fact that we were cousins. Even more importantly, Evelyn was fun, always in a good mood, and, not a tattletale. Given my tendency to be a little bad sometimes (some would argue, a lot bad always), non-tattling was an endearing trait indeed.

Evelyn was very popular, although she was both vertically and hor-izontally challenged. Those of you who are not politically correct and haven't spent much time in suave places like Little Rock or Birmingham might say that she was short and fat. If you had gone to Mrs. Doolittle's Charm School, you certainly wouldn't have said such a thing, but not everybody was so fortunate.

Evelyn was good-natured about her resemblance to a fire plug, fre-quently joking about her weight. She was a good sport when she was nicknamed Skinny-less and even took it calmly when that was later was contracted to Skinless. For the record, she did have skin. Every darn one of my cousins had skin, for that matter, though some more than others. When you consider that some of Evelyn's classmates had nicknames such as Granny, Philip, Goat, Toad, Brainy, Sully, and Coo, I guess Skinless isn't so unusual.

Being built the way she was, Evelyn wasn't exactly what you would call athletic. When we were in the third grade, she came to my house to play one afternoon after school. We were having a great time, but of course I never let well enough alone. Somehow I convinced Evelyn that we could have an even better time if we climbed up on top of the garage.

I don't remember what reason I gave for this. But I kept a ladder nearby, as I tended to spend a lot of time up there. Where better to put on my Superman cape (a pink towel with frayed edges held together with a diaper pin) and leap down on villains such as Lex Luther, once again saving Metropolis (or was that where Batman lived)? Where better to emulate my Saturday afternoon matinees idols like Lash LaRue and Johnny Mac Brown by jumping off the balcony of the saloon, landing straddling my horse, and riding off into the sunset? (I didn't really question it at the time, but later I never could understand how they could jump off of a building and land straddling a horse without doing a real-life version of *The Nutcracker,* or at least having to move up to the tenor section of the choir.)

The edge of the garage roof was eight to ten feet off the ground. That was an easy jump for a boy eight or nine years old, though not exactly in the comfort range of an eight- or nine-year-old girl built like Evelyn was. Feeling the need to show off for my cousin, I went to the edge of the roof and, imitating the sounds of drums rolling and trumpets blaring, jumped to the ground with ease.

Evelyn wasn't particularly impressed. Certainly, she showed not the slightest inclination to follow suit. I climbed the ladder and jumped again, and again, and again, each time coaxing her to jump as well. But neither that, a dare, nor even the never-failing double-dog dare worked. Evelyn still steadfastly refused. "I don't care what you say, I'm not going to do it!" she repeated several times.

Growing more and more frustrated, I suddenly remembered something. I had felt the same reluctance before my good friend Erskine McLemore coaxed me into my own first jump. It seemed logical to use the same method with her that he had used with me.

"I promise, you're gonna love it," I said.

And then I removed the ladder.

Evelyn pleaded with me to replace it. But, convinced I was helping her conquer her fear, I refused. After about thirty minutes, she realized there was no one about to come to her rescue and that darkness was falling fast. After her sweet, loving cousin—yes, that would be me—threatened to go into the house and leave her all alone, she finally decided to jump. I think she was about halfway down when I began to wonder if this had been one of my better ideas. There just wasn't much about Evelyn's leap that would have been considered graceful. Even to my inexperienced eyes, the sight of her thick little body falling through the air did not look good.

To her credit, she landed flat on both feet, though with a rather loud thud. Both of her ankles more or less immediately "swole up," as we put it at the time. In mere seconds they grew to the size of a prize cantaloupe at the Hinds County Fair and took on the color of two huge black eyes. Evelyn looked pitiful sitting on the ground, crying and nursing her basketball-sized, bluish-black ankles. I encouraged her to cry a little more softly so as not to get us in trouble, but for some reason that only made her cry more.

I coaxed Evelyn to get up, to no avail. I tried to help her, also to no avail. For some strange reason, she wasn't the least bit interested in my helping her. I know you will find it difficult to imagine anyone being this unappreciative.

Time being a-wasting, I would soon be called in for dinner. Thinking hard, I surveyed my options. I could, of course, shoot her and put her out of her misery. This had the appeal of being the way any self-respecting cowboy in the Saturday afternoon matinee at the Pix Theater would have solved the dilemma of a horribly wounded animal. But the BB gun would probably not have done the job and it would be difficult explaining to Mama just why I needed Daddy's German Luger. I also wasn't sure what to do with Evelyn once I had "put her out of her misery." They never showed that part at the matinees. Finally, I knew that her mom would come around and ask a lot of questions. "Honest, Aunt Ruby, I don't know where she is," I imagined myself saying. "She climbed up this giant beanstalk that went into the sky and just disappeared. Really, she did. Cross my heart and hope to…

er, never mind." Sadly, I knew Aunt Ruby would never believe me. Jackie had seen to that.

If only 911 had been available back then, I could have just put in a call and gone on in for supper. But since the EMS system had not been developed yet, I didn't seem to have any choice but to tell Mama what had happened.

After doing so, I was sorry I had not explored the "putting her out of her misery" scenario a little further. It also grew clear that it would have been easier to deal with Aunt Ruby than my mother, who quickly looked like she needed a straitjacket application followed by electroshock therapy.

I had been unsuccessful at helping Evelyn up, and Mama wasn't having much luck either. Evelyn couldn't bear even the slightest weight on her ankles, which by now were bigger and blacker than ever. After Mama somehow managed to get her into the house, she began soaking Evelyn's ankles in a tub of hot Epson salts water. I don't recall that remedy from medical school, but maybe I was absent that day.

To compound the problem, we did not own a car. Flatfoot, the Fondren family car, had been sold after the death of my grandparents. Mama finally used Uncle Snooks's vehicle to take Evelyn home. She then had to explain what her boneheaded son had done. Fortunately, Aunt Ruby had a son of her own, Tootie, who wasn't exactly an angel himself. That may have made it a little bit easier for Aunt Ruby to understand how a boy might come to do such a dumb thing.

Despite this unfortunate act on my part, Evelyn and I remained fast friends. We lost touch over the years once our homes were separated by an entire continent. Evelyn became very successful, first as a career Navy nurse and later as a tour director in San Francisco. She was said to have established the first ever walking tour in that city, so I guess her ankles must have eventually recovered.

As I began writing these recollections, I realized how foolish it was to have lost contact with this dear friend and relative. I decided to e-mail her an invitation to come to Atlanta to become reacquainted. Unfortunately, I never did so. I was lucky enough to see Evelyn one final time at a family reunion in Jackson. She looked great, but she passed away not too long afterward.

I wish I had had the chance for a longer visit with her. I think we could have had a lot fun. Who knows, I might have even taken her up on the roof.

Sisters

I QUITE LITERALLY OWE MY LIFE TO GLADYS, MY OLDER SISTER. Had she not been such a sweet, loving person, she would have killed me well before I reached the age of five. Absolutely no one would have blamed her, at least no one who knew us well.

There are only two reasons I can offer as to why Gladys didn't carry out my assassination. First of all, she just plain wasn't spiteful enough. I had apparently received all of those genes. And secondly, she wasn't athletic enough. It takes some degree of athleticism to stab, bludgeon, hang, or even shoot someone and poor Gladys did not have it. She was the only person I have ever known who feared going to a grammar school birthday party where she might have to play "Ring Around the Rosie."

Despite her lack of athletic ability (not to mention her total lack of desire to go) Gladys was sent to Camp Montreat in the mountains of North Carolina for one month when she was thirteen. When you lived in Mississippi in the 1940s, going to the North Carolina mountains was a really big deal, so I envied her journey to camp immensely. By then I had almost run out of opportunities to make trouble at home. (Almost, but not quite.) Moreover, I actually *did* have the athletic ability required to play "Ring Around the Rosie." I also did very well at "Pin the Tail on the Donkey" (especially once I figured out how to peek around the blindfold.) Why in the world my parents decided to send her to camp will always be a mystery to me. In contrast, when I was twelve I got to go to Camp Kickapoo, which was exactly eight miles outside of Jackson, and only for a single lousy week. The authorities not wanting to let me out of their jurisdiction may have played some small part in that.

When Gladys arrived at camp, she was greeted with all kinds of activities that held very little interest for her, including swimming, hiking, softball, volleyball, and, especially, sack races. One afternoon as she walked to the mess hall, she noticed an isolated cabin with white curtains gently blowing in the wind. Three beds, each with two pillows, were lined up within it, and a little flower vase sat by each bed. Naturally, Gladys was curious. When she inquired, she was told it was "the Clinic," and used for campers who did not feel well.

Now, Gladys wasn't usually devious—I got all of those genes, too. But she knew that camp was an unusual situation, which called for drastic measures. The following morning, after breakfast and before the sack race, she walked to the Clinic, reporting that she was feeling sick to her stomach. The response was immediate. A caring and compassionate nurse tucked Gladys into one of the beds and gave her a *Seventeen* magazine to read. It was all so peaceful and pleasant that my sister almost drifted off to sleep. Then she noticed the nurse busying herself right beside the bed. When Gladys asked what she was doing, the nurse she said she was preparing an enema. Gladys quickly looked around the clinic. Not seeing anyone else there, she asked whom the enema was for. Smiling, the kind nurse continued her preparation, explaining that anyone who came to the clinic for the day got an enema.

Gladys may have lacked athletic ability, but the nurse later reported that she had never seen anyone leap out of bed or sprint to swimming class with such speed and enthusiasm. From that day on she was very enthusiastic about all camp activities, even the daily sack race.

Gladys wasn't my only sister, of course. I was five when Mama explained to me that she and Daddy had asked God to give them a baby and that I would soon be having another sibling. Ecstatic, I started jumping around, yelling that I couldn't wait until my little brother was born. I had always wanted a brother and now I was going to get one. "This is gonna be great! When can we go pick him out?"

I knew all about babies. To get a baby, a lady had to go to the Baptist Hospital. I didn't know why, but that didn't make any difference. Just like you had to go to the hardware store to get nails and to the grocery store to get eggs, you went to the Baptist Hospital to get babies. I didn't care about the details. I figured we should just get it over with and go pick him up.

To the extent I pictured the process in any more detail, I figured it went something like this. The lady wanting a baby went somewhere inside the hospital, maybe the cafeteria, while a nurse went outside to wait for the baby. The baby would then come down a long sliding board that started in heaven (duh) and ended up at the side entrance. The nurse had to be there to catch him, otherwise he could land on the concrete sidewalk, roll out into the street, and get hit by a car. After she caught the baby, the nurse would take him inside and give him to the mother, so the mother could get home and fix supper.

But five minutes into my celebration, right about the time I started thinking about what my brother's name should be, Mama said there was something we needed to talk about. As you know, I hated it when she said there was something we needed to talk about. But I hadn't done anything bad in at least the last few minutes, so I wasn't all that worried.

She sat me down and sat across from me. "God is going to give us a baby, but it will take a few months, and it may be a girl," she said.

The timing didn't really concern me, but the girl part did. "What? Why in the world would He give us a girl if he knows we want a boy?" I asked indignantly.

"God will give us what He wants us to have, and we have to be thankful for whatever He gives us."

"That's the dumbest thing I ever heard of," I retorted. "If He's going to give us a baby, why wouldn't he give us what we want? That's like asking for a cap pistol and getting a doll instead! It's just plain stupid!"

Mama then explained in no uncertain terms that we *never* questioned what God thought best and that we *would* be delighted with whatever He gave us. It was quite obvious from her tone that this conversation was over, that I was treading on thin ice, and that any further discussion of the matter was likely to held in the Hoorah Patch.

Over the next few months Mama, Daddy, and all my relatives kept reminding me how lucky I would be to get a little sister. By the time Mary Agnes finally arrived, I was therefore resigned to the idea. But I did notice a lot of things seemed to change, and not entirely for the better.

First of all, Mama did not just go to the hospital, pick up the baby, and come home and fix supper. As a matter of fact, she stayed there about a week and then came home in an ambulance. After that, she didn't fix supper for a long time. To make matters worse, she just stayed in bed and spent all of her time with that little baby. To my mind she spent very little time with me, and nobody else did either. In retrospect I'm sure that perception wasn't true, but it certainly seemed to be at the time.

On Sunday afternoon, I found myself really bored. Fed up with the total lack of attention, I decided to go into the kitchen and make a glass of chocolate milk. I had just gotten the milk bottle out of the icebox when I realized that someone had made a terrible mistake. They had bought Bosco® syrup instead of Hershey's. I thought everybody knew better than that. You had to use much more of Bosco. That day, I think I decided on one third of a glass of Bosco to two-thirds of a glass of milk. It still wasn't very good, and it got much worse about thirty minutes later when I threw it all up. The untimely regurgitation, combined with my decision to spread the rest of the Bosco syrup all over the kitchen table in protest, did finally result in my getting a little attention, though I wouldn't say it was exactly the kind of attention I craved.

Despite my disappointment over the lack of a brother, Mary Agnes turned out to be a neat little kid. Everyone agreed she was as "good as gold." You never heard a peep out of her, at least until her brother came home from school and began to aggravate her. Since there were five years between us, we never really played together. And she was, after all, a girl. Charming as she could be, she wasn't worth a hoot at wrestling or playing cowboys.

Though she was too young to play with, Mary Agnes wasn't too young to tease. I made fun of her and our cousin Patty for most of their childhood. I am sure they both dreaded the sight of me, so they pretty much kept their distance. Mary Agnes and I never actually fought, but we just did not seem to have much in common. Mary Agnes had a lot of friends and so did I, and we pretty much went our separate ways.

Until, that is, one day at Boy Scout camp. I was at good ol' Camp Kickapoo, and we were resting after working hard at making lariats, tying knots, woodcarving, and learning to start fires without matches. (The latter was actually not too hard if you were able sneak in your old man's Zippo lighter.) I was on the top bunk of our cabin, with the other boys on other beds and the floor.

Somehow we got around to talking about our younger siblings. "My little sister can really drive me crazy," I said without thinking.

"Boy, that's the truth!" chimed in a friend who will remain nameless. "I was over at Billy's house last week, and she drove us nuts."

I knew immediately that while it might be okay for *me* to talk about my sister, it sure as heck was *not* okay for anyone else to talk about her. This realization became even more apparent as I leapt off of the top bunk and punched my pal in the nose. I remember having a hard time explaining why I was so upset with someone who had done nothing but agree with me.

This incident made a big impression on me. I don't think I ever thought of Mary Agnes the same way again. I began to think of myself as her protector, and despite my earlier torture of her, she began to think of me that way too. One day when she was in the fourth grade she told me about two boys, a couple of years older, who had stopped her while she was riding her bicycle. They were very mean to her, frightening her by describing the horrible things they would do to her if she ever rode by their house again. Saying nothing about this to Mary Agnes, the following day I went to their classroom at Duling School. I knew the teacher well, as I had been one of her pupils a few years earlier. I asked if I might talk in the hall to two of her students. Surprisingly, she allowed me to do so.

Of course, I was much older than these boys. I'm sure I scared them much worse than they scared Mary Agnes, in part by describing in vivid detail the anatomical changes that would take place if they *ever* so much as looked in my sister's direction. To the best of my knowledge, they never did.

I became very close to both of my sisters as we grew older, a closeness that has deepened with each passing year. Equally delightful, they are both always in a good mood, with big smiles and bigger hearts. I can say with absolute sincerity that you just couldn't have more wonderful sisters than Gladys and Mary Agnes. So I'm glad after all that they made it down the slide at the Baptist Hospital—and even more grateful that neither of them landed on the concrete, rolled into the street, and got hit by a car.

The Brownie Dress

*F*ROM THE STORIES I HAVE TOLD SO FAR, YOU MIGHT HAVE begun to think that I was a rather mischievous child. On the contrary, I think I was actually a very good boy who was faced with temptations no child could resist. At least, so it was with the lipstick and the Brownie dress.

It was a beautiful spring afternoon. Having been cooped up all winter, I had not gotten into any real trouble for a week or so. Well, at least not for the last few hours. So when I spied the tube of lipstick on the sidewalk in front of Fondren Grocery Store, I quickly picked it up and put it in my pocket. I wasn't sure just what I could do with it or why a boy would even want such a thing. I sure as heck wasn't planning on putting it on my own lips. I just thought it might come in handy for *something*.

I was playing with George Sanders that afternoon. George was a couple of years older than I and lived a few doors down the street. When I spotted the lipstick, we were swinging on the horizontal bar that supported the awning across the front of the store. The bar was about seven feet above the ground. We would climb up on the ledge in front of the store window, jump out onto the bar, swing by our hands, and then hang upside down by our knees. I am not sure why Aunt May permitted these shenanigans. I suspect she thought it better for me to be out there rather than wreaking havoc inside her store. Yes, now that I think about it I'm quite sure that must have been the reason.

"What'cha gonna do with that girlie stuff?" George asked as I pocketed the lipstick tube.

"I dunno," I replied. "We could use it to write something on the window." George pointed out that Aunt May was watching us. So for the time being, I just kept the lipstick in my pocket.

As the afternoon rolled on, George and I ended up playing on top of a dirt mound. The mound lay behind Fondren Presbyterian Church, which at that time was next door to the grocery store. After a while, Ms. Thigpen and her two daughters came walking by on their way home from the store. George and I hid behind the mound, circling it carefully so that it was always between us and them.

They were just strolling along, talking about whatever it is that little girls and their mothers talk about. It was probably something angelic, like the pretty curled hair of the new Sunday school teacher. Those same little curls had gotten me into trouble when I yanked one of them as she stood up to sing in prayer meeting the Wednesday night before, but that's another story.

Ms. Thigpen and one of the girls had on sweaters, as the day was still rather crisp. The daughter walking between them, whose name I've long forgotten, had on her brand-new Brownie uniform. As I looked at the back of the uniform—so starched, so crisp and so clean—I knew immediately what I wanted to do with the lipstick. Damn... er, I mean, darn, I'm glad I had the foresight not to let the opportunity slip by.

I explained to George that I was going to sneak up behind the trio and color on the back of the Brownie dress. George—being two years older than I and having the benefit of two extra years of maturity, experience, wisdom and, no doubt, punishments—thought deeply as he pondered my proposal.

After considering every aspect of the plan for approximately six seconds, he announced that he thought it was a swell idea. I discovered that day how wonderful it is to have the support of an older colleague, someone who has your best interests at heart and would never, ever lead you astray.

With the stealth of a leopard that had just spotted his unsuspecting dinner grazing in the tall grass, with the help of my black high-top Converse tennis shoes and while maintaining a low crouch, I cautiously inched my way up behind the Thigpens, falling right in behind them in a way that would have made even the most sly and insidious Indian Scout proud. I remember looking up at Mrs. Thigpen's profile. To this day I can't imagine how she did not glimpse me out of the corner of her eye.

Trying not to laugh as I listened to them chatter, I slowly reached into my pocket and retrieved the prized lipstick. I took off the top, returned it to my pocket, then twisted the case until the lipstick reached maximum length. Not being much of an artist, I didn't draw any cartoon characters, nor did I write anything clever. I just lightly and very softly scribbled all over the back of the dress. Then I slowed my pace to let the three women pull away from me.

With all that done, I ran back toward George, still hiding behind the mound. He was initially delighted with the results of my endeavor. However, I think his maturity, experience, and wisdom finally did kick in. At that point he decided that being with me the rest of the afternoon might not be wise. Or perhaps he suddenly developed a keen interest in studying the equilateral triangle or pinpointing the source of the Nile. At any rate, he did an immediate exit, stage left, and ran all the way home.

As usual after such a stunt, my conscience got the best of me. About twelve minutes later, I made my way home to tell my mother about the latest mess her obstreperous son had created for her. I'm sorry for her sake that tranquillizers were not easy to find at the time and that, being a teetotaler in a state where liquor was illegal, she couldn't even resort to a stiff drink.

She needed it badly, that was immediately clear. "You did *what*?" she yelled. "I don't believe you. They would have seen you or heard you—you're not exactly quiet. They would have seen you, and that's all there is to it!"

Bless her heart, she had almost convinced herself. But when I pulled out the worn-down tube of lipstick, she knew I had let her down again. With a trembling hand and a tear in her eye, she called Ms. Thigpen, looking for, and praying not to find, confirmation of what I had told her.

As it transpired, Mrs. Thigpen had already punished her own innocent daughter for ruining the Brownie uniform, which had cost a full thirteen dollars. It was now in the wash, but if the lipstick did not come out, Mama volunteered to buy a replacement. When my mother hung up, her face was grim. Turning to me, she began explaining through clenched teeth just how long it would take me to reimburse her for $13.00 with my meager weekly allowance.

There were some very anxious moments over the next couple of hours, which seemed like a couple of days. I used the time trying very hard to figure out how I could slip through the cracks of the hardwood floor, while Mama, I think, was trying to decide if it would be better to face her maker after committing suicide, or the judge after committing juvenile homicide. At least the latter would likely be ruled justifiable.

When Mama called Ms. Thigpen some hours later for an update, she was told that all of the lipstick had come out in the wash. Though this was the best news possible, neither of us was rejoicing. With "my tail between my legs," I quietly went to my room. And while I can't be sure, I have always suspected that Mama went somewhere for a good stiff drink.

The Pix Theater

*W*HEN I WAS A KID, THE COST OF A TICKET AT THE PIX THEATER was fifteen cents, and a box of popcorn cost ten cents. (The same size box now costs more than a bicycle did back then.) I'm sure Mama must have thought this the best value she got for her money all week. Where else, indeed, could you get a baby-sitting service for six cents an hour with no worry about the safety of your children or the suitability of what they would be viewing?

The Pix was very small by today's standards, with a lone ticket booth and a refreshments counter that sold popcorn and very little else. From the foyer, a single door led into the theater. Features changed frequently: a movie would play Monday through Wednesday, then a new feature would show Thursday, Friday, and Saturday nights. The Pix was nothing short of bedlam during the children's matinee on Saturday afternoons, when it was packed with loud-talking kids. I'm sure the theater had a special crew to come in after the matinee to hose all the bubble gum off of the seats before the adults came in on Saturday nights. There were no shows on Sunday until the mid 1960s, when everything started to change. Stores started to open on Sundays then, theaters like the Pix started playing movies on the Lord's Day, and some people even began to mow their lawns and wash their cars even though it was supposed to be a day of rest.

All movies then were in black and white, of course. There wasn't any profanity and certainly no sex. Polite folks did not even use that term. If the word "sex" was used back then, it was to inquire if an infant were male or female. Fortunately, you didn't have to put up with a lot of kissing either. During the years when I went to the Pix weekly I thought there was nothing more disgusting than going to a good cowboy movie and seeing some cowboy singing songs and kissing girls instead of shootin' and fightin'. I called those foolish fellows "singing cowboys" and did my absolute best to avoid them.

While cowboy movies were full of fistfights and gunplay, there was never any real violence, by today's standards anyway—no buckets of blood, no brains or intestines splattered across the screen. People (mostly bad guys) were shot in the abdomen, whereupon they would bend over, clutch at their wounds and instantly fall dead. Not just the level of violence but the finality of cinematic death has changed since then. Since the success of *Fatal Attraction* and *The Terminator*, nobody stays dead anymore. It is now necessary for the villains to be killed over and over, each time more violently than the last. I swear, some of today's bad guys have more lives than a cross between an alley cat and a cockroach.

The Pix's Saturday lineup was always the same. The highlight was the double feature. I always hoped that at least one of the movies (we didn't call them "films" yet) wouldn't have a cowboy who sang songs. If Roy Rogers, Gene Autry, and Eddie Dean were involved, you could bet your popcorn you were going to have more singing than fightin' and more kissing than shootin'. On the other hand, movies that featured Johnny Mac Brown, Alan "Rocky" Lane, or the Lone Ranger had no songs to worry about. Probably, none of them could have carried a tune in a watering trough.

In addition to the double feature, there was always a serial. In each episode, the star would be shown narrowly escaping the certain death that had loomed at the end of the previous week's episode, only to find himself in another death trap by the end of the current one. There would also be a short feature such as *The Three Stooges*, *The Little Rascals*, or *The Bowery Boys*; a cartoon; and a newsreel. From my point of view, the newsreel was a real good time to go to the bathroom, get some more popcorn, or maybe ask the girl I was currently pretending not to like if it was okay if I held her hand. This lineup of entertainment would take up the entire afternoon.

There was a definite predictability to the movies at the Pix. The villains "whipped" and outsmarted the good guys at the start but right always won out over might in the end. You could depend on that. The good guys either rode white horses or wore white hats, and their hats never came off even though they fought in barroom brawls, fell off horses, and jumped off cliffs into raging rivers. To be entirely accurate, I have to admit that some of the good guys wore black, including the Durango Kid, Hopalong Cassidy, Zorro, and Lash LaRue. Lash was my all-time favorite. He carried a whip, he sang not a single song, and he never, ever thought about kissing girls. In my early years at the Pix, he was my kind of guy.

Thanks to the similarity from picture to picture, the lessons of these movies were easy to learn. With the exception of my family and the Fondren Presbyterian Church, there were few things growing up in Jackson that influenced me more than what I saw at the Pix Theater. Women, elders and children were to be respected. Bullies who abused and mistreated others lost out in the end. Heroes like Sergeant York, Babe Ruth, Dizzy Dean, and Lou Gehrig were ordinary people from humble backgrounds who overcame impossible odds through sheer determination and perseverance. I'm grateful to this day for the lessons I learned there, except maybe for the one about the bad guys dressing differently from the good ones. In real life, of course, villains can look pretty much like everyone else, which makes life very complicated.

Accuracy, unlike virtue, was definitely not at a premium in those pictures. Tarzan frequently fought tigers in the African jungle, even though there aren't any tigers in Africa, and battled sharks and octopuses, both sea creatures, in the Congo River. The huge, man-eating plants with which he had dangerous encounters are also pretty much nonexistent. Johnny Weissmuller, a former Olympic swimmer, played the part of Tarzan until he became so overweight he looked ridiculous in his loincloth. At that time he became Jungle Jim, another character who had to deal with the same nonexistent African animals and man-eating plants. Accurate or not, I never had to worry about Jungle Jim or Tarzan kissing girls or singing songs. Tarzan, in fact, could barely talk. Mostly, he grunted one-syllable words and short phrases: "Me Tarzan, you Jane." "You cook, me eat."

Though I didn't understand it at the beginning, another African picture foreshadowed my maturing sense of the kind of pleasures that the Pix offered. It was *Nyoka the Jungle Girl*. I might have been anti-kissing in general, but I could easily understand why somebody might want to kiss *her*. I didn't know what "sexy" was at that time, but that is exactly what she was. She wore an outfit that looked like someone had stretched one of Tarzan's loincloths upward in such a way as to cover her …well, you know. We didn't really talk about those things back then, although I sure spent a lot of time thinking about those … well, you know.

Eventually, my interest in Nyoka extended to real girls. I had my first dates at the Pix Theater. Peggy Price was my first real girlfriend. A beautiful blond whose family had bought our house on Mitchell Street when we moved to the Big House, she really stole my heart.

I asked her to join me at the Pix, but when I met her in front of the theater I became completely flustered. All of the other guys in my class were standing in line together, none of them with girls. Thinking quickly,

I inconspicuously slipped Peggy a quarter, instructed her under my breath to purchase her own ticket and popcorn, and whispered that she should meet me inside. I felt proud of the way I had avoided letting my friends think me interested in a mere girl. I'm not sure why I thought they wouldn't notice the fact that I was sitting by her and holding her moist little hand.

As I said, Mama enthusiastically supported my love for the Pix and saw to it that I went to almost every matinee. In all of those years, I can remember missing only two Saturday afternoons there. Once I had a really bad case of the whooping-measles, or maybe the chicken-mumps. I can't really remember the illness, just that it was a terrible time to be sick. The final episode of *Nyoka the Jungle Girl* was showing that afternoon. Did I mention earlier that it would have been okay to kiss Nyoka, especially if I was the one who got to do the kissing?

I was absolutely crushed to miss the end of the story. Even if my friends had been allowed to come into my sickroom, there was no way I could wait for them to finish the entire afternoon before coming to give me the gist. I raised such a fuss that my Uncle Bob, bless his heart, finally agreed to go to the Pix, see the serial and head home immediately with the outcome. This was a tremendous sacrifice for Uncle Bob, as no adult in his right mind would even vaguely consider going to the Pix on a Saturday afternoon.

As soon as the episode was over, he came straight to my sickbed with a full report. I can't actually remember the ending that carried such earthshaking importance at the time. But I do still remember how Nyoka looked in her …er …well, never mind.

The other time I failed to get to the Pix on Saturday, I had accepted an invitation from Uncle Snooks and Aunt May to go fishing. We left early one summer morning. I didn't really know what day it was. During the summer, all the days tended to run together. I rarely knew one from the other unless my mother was giving me a quarter for the matinee or scrubbing my ears for Sunday school. Anyway, all things considered, I was having a reasonable time on the trip. I did find the small boat a little confining. I also thought it a little stupid to sit there for hours hoping a fish would bite my hook, especially when I couldn't see a single fish in the entire lake.

Then Uncle Snooks said something about church the following day. I realized with horror that it was in fact Saturday. Asking him the time, I was told that one o'clock was fast approaching.

Sitting in a boat in the middle of that lake, many miles from home, I quickly figured out that I wouldn't make it to the Pix that afternoon. I was thrown into despair. How could this possibly have happened, I wondered miserably. Why didn't Mama, Aunt May, or the tooth fairy stop me from making such a terrible mistake? I was only a little kid, but they should have known better. Missing Saturday afternoon at the Pix was an awful fate, one that I wasn't sure I could survive.

I remember becoming very quiet, which did not happen very often, and feeling distinctly queasy. I suppose that I must have looked rather pale because Aunt May looked at me sympathetically and asked, "Billy, are you homesick?"

"N'ome," was my indignant reply, "I ain't homesick. I'm picture show sick!"

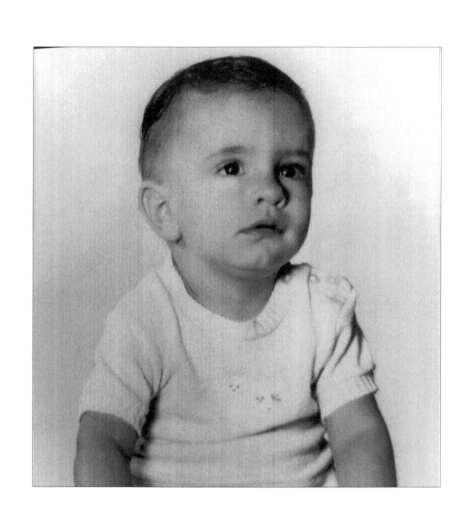

This One's Gotta Be a Boy

*O*NE MORNING WHEN I WAS NINE, MAMA SAID SHE HAD SOME-
thing important to tell me. Since she phrased it that way, as
opposed to "There's something I need to talk to you about," I didn't
feel personally threatened. However, I already knew what this was all
about. You see, when I had found a half-pint of whiskey in Daddy's
car a few days before, I had cautiously explained to Mama that Daddy
was obviously an alcoholic. She had defended him, but now I reckoned
she had decided to tell me the truth after all.

"About Daddy's drinking?" I asked.

"What? Oh, no." Once again she told me not to worry about Daddy.
"Anyway," she went on, "there is something very important that I need
to tell you, but you must promise you won't tell a soul. Do you promise
not to tell *anyone*, if I tell you?" I reluctantly agreed. Then she blurted
out that she was going to have a baby.

Wow! That *was* important news. "Why is it a secret?" I asked.

Mama seemed to be flustered by this question. "There are some
things you don't understand. But I don't have time to explain right
now." She was just sitting and shelling peas, but maybe that was more
demanding than I realized.

Boy, there sure seemed to be a lot of confusing stuff about having babies. One thing I did know for sure, however. I wasn't going to ask anything about whether it would be a boy or a girl. I had learned from the birth of Mary Agnes that we had to take whatever God gave us and be thankful for it. But, between you and me, I also knew something else. God had tricked me once, but he wouldn't do it again. I just knew I was going to have a brother. As this proves, though many people in Jackson saw me as the spawn of the Devil, I was really quite a spiritual child.

Although Mama gained about fifty pounds with that pregnancy, I kept my promise and didn't tell a soul. I was quite tempted to tell Daddy, however. Quite frankly, I thought he should know.

Several months later, we all went to Aunt Ag's house in Edwards, Mississippi, for Sunday dinner. Mama had grown fairly enormous by then, but being with her every day, I never noticed the change. She just looked like Mama to me. I never really gave it a thought.

There just wasn't much to do in Edwards back then. Of course, times have changed. Now if you go to Edwards, you can watch television. Bored silly, five or six of us cousins decided to do the most exciting thing there was to do in Edwards at the time, which was to walk the half-mile down the railroad tracks to downtown, where all the activity was. There was a gas station in town that stayed open on Sundays, and it had a cooler filled with Coca-Cola, Orange Crush, and RC Cola. As if that weren't enough, you could get gum and candy too. I bet some people live their entire life without being exposed to this much excitement.

I was five years younger than my sister Gladys and my cousin Dave, and at least ten years younger than the rest of the group. As we ambled along, everyone had something to say that got the group's attention except me. I was being pretty much ignored.

"I know a secret," I said when there was a lull in the conversation. "If you promise not to tell, I'll tell you what it is."

They agreed. Quietly, I whispered that my mama was going to have a baby.

"What do you mean?" Dave asked.

"I mean my mama is going to have a baby," I said, confused.

"Is that all? What's the rest of the story?"

"That's all. Just please don't tell anybody. I never should have told you."

For a few seconds, everything got very quiet. The cousins looked at each other, and then at me, before the guffaws started. Two of them bent over like they were going to throw up, and all of them laughed like it was the funniest thing they had ever heard.

"Why, Billy," Sonny said, "that's absolutely the biggest secret I have heard since they told me the world wasn't flat." I did not have a clue why everyone was laughing and I wasn't sure which I was more, embarrassed or confused, but I sure knew that I didn't like it.

Around that time, Mama had a bad fall. There was a question as to whether she would "lose the baby." I don't know how far along she was, but she went into labor much earlier than expected. I was working at the grocery store that Saturday. This was of course before the time when scores of people including boyfriends, the kids and the folks from down the block and pets waited at the hospital or even piled into the delivery room with popcorn and video cameras.

Sitting in the waiting room smoking one Chesterfield after another, Daddy would periodically call Aunt May. The phone at the store would ring, and Aunt May would shout out a progress report. Finally, she looked over and called, "Billy, you have a baby brother!"

"Okay," I called back, sweeping industriously away for reasons already explained.

"*Okay?* Aren't you excited that it's a boy?"

"Not really. I knew it was a boy all along," I said nonchalantly.

"*And* just how did you know that?" she asked indignantly.

"'Cause I knew God wasn't going to trick me twice," I replied quietly but knowingly. She looked askance at that, but she didn't argue.

My little brother, Richard, was almost ten years younger than I. We therefore never played together, but he was a great little kid, and we had fun.

Richard had a severe hearing loss that required hearing aids in both ears. So did our cousin, Ken Goodrich, who was close to Richard's age. This challenge didn't seem to curb them much. They were quite a pair, constantly stirring up all sorts of mischief.

As Ken said later, it was many years before he was able to figure out the reason that he and Richard were always caught so quickly while making mischief. It didn't matter whether they were trying to sneak out after bedtime, smoke some cigarettes they lifted from Daddy's pack, or sneaking a peek at a "men's magazine," Daddy or one of Ken's folks was always right there to catch them in the act.

The problem was that their conversations usually went something like this.

"PSST. YOU WANNA SNEAK OUTTA THE HOUSE AND GO DOWN TO THE CREEK?" Richard would "whisper."

"YEAH, SURE. BUT IT'S FOUR O'CLOCK IN THE MORNING!"

"YEAH. LET'S BE CAREFUL SO WE DON'T GET CAUGHT."

Naturally, some adult was always standing there waiting for them before they even get out of the door. Ken insists that he was at least twenty-two before he ever heard Daddy say anything other than "What do you boys think you're doing?" No matter how deaf they both were, they always managed to hear that remark.

One of their more memorable moments occurred one night when Ken was staying over at our house. He and Richard were supposed to be sleeping in the living room. Instead, Richard challenged him to a contest in which they would both take a large mouthful of water, open their mouth and insert an Alka-Seltzer. The idea was to see who could hold it the longest before it exploded. They had just both put an Alka-Seltzer in their mouth when Daddy entered the room and asked his usual question: "What do you boys think you're doing?"

Richard managed to swallow his tablet. Despite the explosion surely going on in his stomach, he nonchalantly answered, "Nothin'." But Ken started to laugh, expelling more or less equal amounts of Alka-Seltzer fizz out of his mouth, his ears, and his nose.

Fortunately for them, Daddy wasn't too surprised at this, or anything else they did. By then I think he had just about seen it all.

Their antics, and possibly some of mine, gave Ken good sermon material for the Presbyterian minister that he later became. He also wrote about this incident in his story, "Dick and Me." It appears in the Fondren Family memories book, *Sweet Peas and Pink Layer Cake*, edited and published by Rob McKibben. Rob is a grandson of Aunt Margaret and Uncle Bob, but if you can't keep all of these cousins straight, you won't be the first one.

With the ten-year difference in our age, Richard and I were not particularly close while growing up. During much of his childhood, I was away at college, medical school, internship, residency, and finally the Air Force. However, once we were grown up my good friend Tom Koch talked Richard into coming to Atlanta to work for X-Ray of Georgia, where he stayed for over 29 years. Since then Richard has worked for the Gwinnett and now the DeKalb Hospital System.

I am grateful to have my brother living close to me, so that we can spend time together. We play golf, vacation together, and share a lot of meals at home and at our favorite restaurant, the Waffle House. I sincerely hope that someday I can become half the man Richard seems to think I am. Sadly, I doubt that will be possible.

The Luger

MY FATHER OWNED A GERMAN LUGER. SUPPOSEDLY, HIS Uncle Luther had taken it off of a German. I'm not sure if this was after the Germans were defeated in some great battle or if he simply picked the man's pocket. I don't even know who Uncle Luther was. For all I know he was one of the extraordinary military minds of that time that I don't remember because I was playing hooky the day we finished up with Eisenhower, MacArthur, Alexander, Napoleon, and got on to Luther.

The gun was large, especially for my small hand; heavy; and, as I would find out, very hard to control. I don't think you could hit a hippo in the butt with a German Luger, even if you were only ten feet away. The gun used a nine-millimeter shell. That would probably bring down the aforementioned hippo if you hit him, but as I just said, you wouldn't have. I can promise you that if Wyatt Earp and Doc Holliday had been using Lugers, they wouldn't have won the gunfight at the OK Corral. No wonder the Germans lost the war.

Daddy kept the gun on the top shelf. He kept the shells in the clip separated from the gun, but didn't put the gun in locked storage. When I tell this story these days I'm sometimes asked why not. Possibly it was because we did not have locked storage and possibly because the need for gun safety wasn't as widely recognized then as it (sadly) has to be now. Daddy wasn't a hunter or a "gun person." But he was a safety fanatic with regard to power tools and almost everything else, so his lack of caution about gun storage was uncharacteristic.

In other ways, however, he was extremely careful. I was allowed to handle the Luger only in my father's presence, strictly forbidden to go near it otherwise, and told that I would be severely punished should I ever disobey this rule. I promised I would *never* do such a thing. And—knowing that I not only loved him dearly but was usually too scared of him to cross him—Daddy believed me.

Sadly, he shouldn't have. I must confess that any time my parents left me alone, I had the Luger out before the tires of the Buick had left the driveway. I would practice twirling and spinning the pistol like Lash Larue, Roy Rogers, and the Durango Kid—not easy things to do with a Luger—and hone my quick draw in front of the mirror. After gunning down the bad guy, I would blow the smoke from the barrel and ceremoniously re-holster the pistol, in an imaginary holster, of course. For some reason, it never occurred to me to shove the clip into the gun.

Though I had enough sense not actually to shoot the pistol, I did figure out another way to stir up some mischief with the Luger. One Saturday afternoon when I was eleven, I decided it would be interesting to shoot at one of the nine-millimeter shells with my BB gun. Boy genius that I was, I felt that it would make a logical and challenging target. This might not have seemed like such an especially appealing idea ordinarily, but I had not done anything really dumb in at least a couple of days and clearly had some mischief pent up.

I placed the large shell on the floor of the doghouse and proceeded to try to hit it with one of my BBs. Expert marksman that I was, I was unable to do this despite its being only two or three feet away. After multiple misses, I realized that I needed to prop up the BB gun on something to steady it. All I could find was some rusted steel that my father was using for his bumper jack invention. He was constantly redrawing the plans and taking pieces of steel to the machine shop for the next prototype, so there were several choices. Fortunately, I chose a large, flat piece—3/4 of an inch thick and about eighteen inches square—rather than one of the steel rods.

The steel was heavy, but I was able to drag it in front of the doghouse and propped the BB gun on it. Even so, I missed the Luger shell twice more. At this point divine intervention failed me, or rather, I failed it. God was clearly trying to tell me something, but I wasn't listening.

On the third try, the BB hit the bullet, which then discharged. I had somehow expected this to happen, but now I immediately wished it hadn't. The sound of the bullet firing was deafening, and simultaneous with the even louder noise of the bullet striking the steel plate. Just remembering the awful racket that resulted makes my palms sweat to this day.

(In writing this chapter, I did an Internet search for the question, "what happens when you shoot a 9mm bullet with a BB gun." This produced a surprising number of answers, including some depictions on YouTube. It does not comfort me to know that full-grown adults are trying the same crazy experiment I did, nor that they are proud enough to put the results on video.)

The horrible noise woke my father, who had been taking a Saturday afternoon nap. He ran out the back door in his boxer shorts. Rubbing his eyes, trying to clear the cobwebs and looking left toward the street, he yelled "What was that noise? It sounded like gunfire!"

"I …I …I dunno. I didn't hear nothin'," I mumbled.

I was to his right, far enough away from him that he didn't notice that I was trembling and white as a sheet. After a long couple of minutes, Daddy decided that a car had probably backfired, that everything was okay and he could safely return to his nap. I readily agreed. I had absolutely no idea what it meant for a car to backfire. But I was delighted with any explanation plausible enough to get him back inside the house so that I could go somewhere quiet and throw up.

When he was safely back in the house, I went back over to look at the piece of steel. What I saw scared the daylights out of me. It now had a huge dimple of thinned steel about five inches in diameter, the center of which was about the level of my mid-chest. I had not yet spent a lot of time looking at anatomy books, but I knew that my heart was in that vicinity and that by and large, hearts and nine-millimeter bullets don't go together very well. By all rights, my little experiment should have been *au revoir, sayonara, hasta la vista,* and *auf Wiedersehen,* the end of this and all future chapters.

Having lived to tell the tale, I end this chapter on a more serious note than usual. I would never tell anyone whether or not to own a gun. But if you do, I urge you to never trust your children with access either to the firearm or its ammunition. The allure is too strong and a child's understanding of consequences is too small. I was fortunate, and so was my father—I can't even imagine how devastated he would have been had the shell hit me. Your child, and you, may not be so lucky.

Learning to Plan Ahead
(the Boy Scout Way)

AROUND TEN YEARS OF AGE, RESTLESS WITH THE WAYS OF childhood, I **decided it was time to accept the responsibilities of maturity and devote my life to a higher cause.** I considered the priesthood, but not knowing anyone who was Catholic, this seemed out of my reach. So I did the next best thing and joined the Cub Scouts.

I loved the ritual and the high level of discipline of the Scouts. Putting on my crisp blue uniform with pride, I would go straight to Mrs. What's-her-name's house for the weekly meeting. She was a wonderful lady, and I loved her dearly; I just don't happen to remember her name. I do know for an absolute fact that her son, who was in my class at Duling Elementary, was one of my dearest friends. As soon as I can remember who *he* was, I'll be sure to let you know.

At the first den meeting, Mrs. What's-her-name described the routine. There would be weekly meetings, which would begin with the listing of our good deeds for the past week. I figured that part would be pretty quick, especially in my case. We would then move on to the infinite ways we would better our community. But the thing that captured my attention most at the first meeting was the book describing the different ranks of Cub Scout. Wolf, Bear, and Lion rank each had its own required activities; a parent had to sign a pledge that their boy had done each project satisfactorily. If a boy worked hard and was diligent, we were told, he could receive a badge at each quarterly pack meeting and could become a Lion by the third.

Having now elevated myself to this higher station in life, I no longer concerned myself with previous activities such as painting or destroying stoves, drums, pianos, and Brownie dresses—pastimes in which my talents were never really appreciated anyway. This left me with a lot of time on my hands. I channeled all of my excess energy into my Cub Scout projects. At the first quarterly pack meeting, which was only a few weeks after my first den meeting, I not only received the Wolf Badge but also the Bear and Lion Badges as well. The man giving out the awards said that no one had ever done that before. I am sure some of the relatives and neighbors who had known me for years were nothing short of astonished by my sudden leap out of the Hoorah Patch and onto the awards platform.

Flush with this success, at twelve I joined the Boy Scouts of America, Troop 10, at Fondren Presbyterian Church. Mr. Story, our scoutmaster, was a strict disciplinarian. When I see movies about Marine drill instructors at Parris Island, I think of him. Coddling young Scouts wasn't Mr. Story's way. For example, when there was a campout that brought several troops together, scouts from other troops were driven there by their mommies, who probably gave them a sweet little kiss, a little snack and a note reassuring them that they would duly be picked up at the end of the event. In contrast, Mr. Story had Troop 10 meet at the church and load all of our equipment on wooden back racks. Back packs were for wimps; back *racks* were for real men. We had made the racks using strips of ¼- inch plywood, soaking each strip in the bathtub until it could be bent to the required specifications. The pieces were then put together with rivets. Screws, nails, or bolts were also for wimps; real men used rivets.

Back racks strapped on, we marched in formation the two miles to and from the campground. Though Mr. Story would no doubt say it built character, it was a tiring way to arrive. And as you can imagine, after sleeping on the ground for two nights among scores of other twelve- to sixteen-year-old boys, we were anything but rested for the march back.

Advancing rank in Boy Scouting was more complicated than in the Cubbies. You were awarded a Tenderfoot Badge just for joining. You were then required to accomplish a significant number of projects to become a Second Class Scout and even a more significant number of projects to become a First Class Scout, the latter group including mastery of Morse code. The ranks of Star, Life, and Eagle Scout were attained by gaining multiple merit badges involving a wide variety of categories and complex skills. I have been told that completing all the requirements necessary to attain Eagle Scout rank is tantamount to getting a college education. I don't know if that's true, but it certainly felt like it when I was working my way through them.

Somehow it came to pass that I was the chief cook for Troop 10. Had Mr. Story known me longer, he might have been wise enough not to let me do anything involving knives, fire, and/or the possible corruption of others. One of our most important events was the big Jamboree Campout, which brought together all the troops in the Jackson area. We were to leave the church on Friday afternoon, camp out Friday and Saturday nights, and break camp after dinner on Sunday. You may recall that dinner was the noon meal in Mississippi in the 1940s and 1950s. Sunday dinner being the week's most important meal, I informed my two assistant cooks that we would be having fried chicken for it.

Since neither Mr. Igloo nor Mr. Playmate had yet invented their little coolers, my assistants asked how we were going to keep the chickens cold for almost three days, until we needed them on Sunday morning. I assured them that this would definitely not be a problem. We would carry three live chickens with us, I explained. On Sunday morning I would wring the chickens' necks immediately before we fried them.

If they had looked dubious about the refrigeration problem, my assistants looked even more doubtful now. I explained airily that I had watched my grandmother and Aunt May wring chickens' necks at least a thousand times. Obviously, I assured them, there "weren't nothin' to it!"

Indeed, I had observed this act just about every time chicken was served to and by my family. Going to the chicken coop, the women picked a chicken up by the neck, twirled it around in big circles, and snapped their wrists. Presto, the chicken's head would come right off. The head would then flop on the ground while the body of the chicken kept running around in circles. Hence the expression, "running around like a chicken with his head cut off." It always seemed to me that the body and head were desperately looking for each other. But the running-around phase only lasted a short time. More or less immediately afterward, to my mind, we would all be eating fried chicken. What could possibly be so difficult about that?

I had spent a good two minutes mapping out this careful plan, and my assistants accepted it without any further questions. As usual, however, the devil was in the details—and believe me when I tell you there were a heckuva lot of devils in this plan. I'm sure you understand that the details were mere minor considerations, certainly no problem for a thirteen-year-old Boy Scout. Details, like backpacks and rivets, were for wimps.

In retrospect, it is unbelievable that we were allowed this much leeway in our menu selection. It was an unusual lapse of Mr. Story's vigilance. I don't remember any adult questioning our plan, even when the live chickens began cackling.

The loud clucking began during the march to the campground. Mr. Story always demanded that we march in tight military formation, which carrying chickens made rather difficult. The birds continued to cackle, right through Saturday and into Sunday morning. Fried chicken aside, after two days absolutely everyone in the camp was ready for the cackling to stop.

We rose early on Sunday, getting the fires started and managing breakfast without any great difficulty. Only a few of the pancakes we served were flipped into the dirt, and they were brushed off and placed on the plates before anyone noticed. Our motto soon became, "What they don't know won't hurt them." Fortunately, teenage boys are pretty resilient.

About mid-morning, it was time to begin preparing dinner. My assistants gathered around to watch the neck-wringing. I confidently reached into the cage and pulled out the first chicken, gently placing my right hand around its neck. Only after I started whirling the bird around did it occur to me that I had never actually done this before, and that this might be something of a disadvantage.

After three twirls, I snapped my wrists. Holding the intact but rather lifeless chicken in my hand, I hastened to save face. Sometimes you had to repeat the twirling process twice, I explained. After the third repetition, still trying to maintain my confident tone, I explained that sometimes it was best to use a handy hatchet to gently remove the head.

It then dawned on me that we needed to remove the feathers from the outside of the birds and the guts, if you'll forgive the impolite term, from the inside. These were among the many details I had neither anticipated nor planned for—and unlike the neck-breaking process, I had never even seen these tasks done. I realize that de-feathering and gutting chickens are not subjects you likely wish to read about. Out of kindness and respect for my gentle readers, as well as the writer's own nausea, I will spare you most of the details of what took place between the beheading and the eating of the chicken.

I remembered vaguely that hot water was involved in separating the chicken from the feathers, and we did happen to have a fire going. I instructed my able-bodied assistants to soak the chickens in hot water before pulling out their feathers. Much to my surprise, they actually did what I asked. We had all learned how to remove the "insides" of a fish, and luckily more or less the same process worked on chickens. So far, so good.

I had watched the butchers cut up chickens a thousand times at Fondren Grocery. Just like, say, playing the violin, it had always looked easy. Alas, butchering, like making actual music from a violin, is harder than it looks. We managed to produce drumsticks and wings, but none of the other parts we butchered ended up looking suitable for Sunday dinner.

Using our versatile hatchets as meat cleavers, we continued to chop up the rest of the chickens until we had many small, indistinguishable pieces. These were probably the first-ever chicken nuggets, but Kentucky Fried Chicken's Colonel Sanders never even once said thank you.

My assistants and I we were effusively complimented for this wonderful parting meal. If you have spent any time around teenage boys, you understand that they can eat almost anything, and lots of it. As far as I know, no one required resuscitation, or even hospitalization. I count that as a victory. Neither I nor my assistants took a single bite of the meat. After getting the proper therapy, I was finally able to eat fried chicken again about the time I started college.

Despite the fried chicken snafu, I loved Scouting and benefited greatly from it. It taught me to be trustworthy, loyal, helpful, friendly, courteous, kind, obedient (my wife might question this one, but eleven out of twelve ain't bad), cheerful, thrifty, brave, clean, and reverent. Okay, maybe eleven out of twelve is a stretch. But—as even my wife would agree—I am frequently cheerful, and usually even clean.

As I mentioned earlier, I rapidly obtained rank of Second Class and completed all of the necessary tasks for First Class except one. I had all the merit badges necessary for Star and Life, and even some of those for Eagle. However, for some reason I have never been able to explain to myself, let alone anyone else, I refused to learn the Morse code. At that time in my life I could memorize anything. In fact, I got through countless tests using memorization, so lack of ability wasn't the problem. I can't explain it. I just dug in my heels and refused, without much thought for the consequences.

I deeply regret not only my failure to make Eagle Scout, but also the fact that I failed because of that single arbitrary refusal. This enduring regret has taught me one of the most valuable lessons I have received from Scouting, and also the only painful one that does not involve fried chicken: the lesson that foolish choices can't always be undone. I have many friends who have gone back in later life to do things they wish they had achieved while young. They have finished college, gotten graduate degrees, married the youthful sweetheart they should have married all along, or traveled the world. Sadly, there are no mid-life do-overs in Scouting. Once you reach the age of eighteen, the window of opportunity for becoming an Eagle Scout is forever closed.

I think that becoming an Eagle Scout would have been a tremendous achievement. It requires sustained effort in a diverse group of accomplishments and skills, at a time in a young man's life when he is being pulled in many directions—toward independence, school, sports, and, of course, girls. An Eagle Scout has a kind of well-roundedness rare in a world that rewards specialization.

In my next life I *will* accomplish the goal of becoming an Eagle Scout. Especially since the Morse code is no longer required.

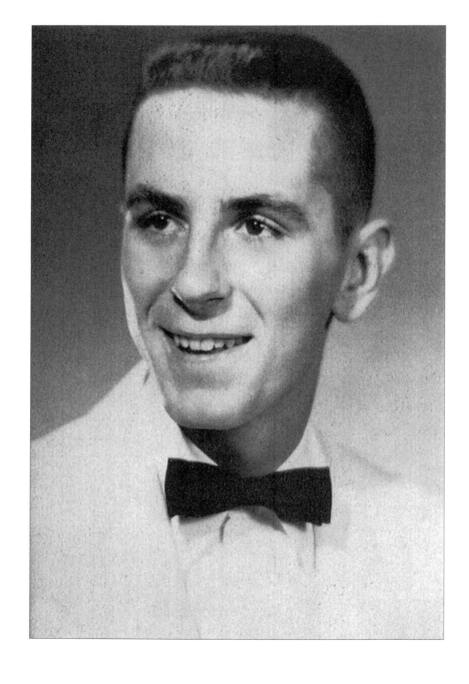

Steve Brasfield

*L*IKE MOST KIDS, I BEGAN TO RELY MORE ON MY FRIENDS AS I grew into adolescence. Steve Brasfield was one of my closest buddies through high school and beyond. We were both good kids who made good grades and came from good families. We were both high school athletes, Steve in basketball and I in football. Both of us were well regarded by the principal and teachers at Murrah High School. We never got into any real trouble. Or, more accurately, we were never caught.

Steve and I both attended Fondren Presbyterian Church. This meant going to Sunday school and church on Sunday and Youth Group meeting on Sunday night. In the Presbyterian Church, youth group was referred to as League. In other churches, the Sunday evening youth group would be called MYF, for the Methodist Youth Fellowship, and BTU, for the Baptist Training Union.

We were upstanding, young, church-going junior citizens. We even frequently went to the evening service. But there was a definite transformation after we left the church on Sunday night. No sooner were we out of the door than we left the path of righteousness and wandered into the valley of mischief and evil. We never made any plans to do anything in particular on these Sunday nights. We didn't need to. It always seemed that the Satan we had been hearing about all day in church was right there waiting for us to come outside and play.

Unwisely, both of our families had given us access to second cars nearly ready for the junkyard. Mama had an old 1949 black Chevrolet, while Steve's mother had a blue Pontiac of approximately the same vintage. We called these rattle traps the "Black Bitch" and the "Blue Bastard." Or was it the "Blue Bitch" and the "Black Bastard"? Time has a way of clouding some of these details. The point is, Steve and I had wheels.

After we left the church, we usually went to the service station to gas up the Black Bitch or Blue Bastard. We would typically buy around twenty-five to forty cents' worth of gas. Gas was around twenty cents a gallon at that time. This being long before the days of self-service, the gas had to be dispensed by an attendant, who would also check your oil and air pressure and wash your windshield.

I know it sounds hard to believe, but sometimes these attendants were or seemed less than thrilled to serve us. Then again, maybe they were just having a bad day. I remember once combining the change in our pockets and asking for thirty-seven cents' worth of regular gasoline. The kindly old gentleman looked disgustedly at Steve and me. Then he looked off to the side. Spitting some tobacco juice on the back tire, he asked, "Do you want me to put all of it in your tank at once or do you want to come back tomorrow and get the rest?"

Not for a moment willing to let this crusty old gentleman have the last word, I gave him my most supercilious look and replied, "What the hell? Go ahead and put it all in tonight. We'll wait!"

One Sunday night in late summer, Steve was driving as we cruised around, minding our own business and waiting on Lucifer to give us our nightly direction. He must not have been on duty that evening, as no instructions were relayed. We had been riding around for at least thirty minutes by then, but couldn't for the life of us find any trouble.

Steve and I discussed trenching the driver education teacher's yard again. But we had done that so many times it was starting to get boring. Then, all of a sudden, I noticed a hammer lying on the floor of Steve's car. I picked it up and got the feel of it in my hand. It had a nice balance. I began to feel right at home with it. After the same careful observation and consideration I always gave such ideas, I suggested to Steve that if he would drive back by that pretty little mailbox with the pink flowers painted on it, I would tap it ever so lightly with the newly found hammer. Steve seemed to think that was a fine idea, and even though Satan had the night off I seemed to hear him agree.

On the first pass, Steve did not get close enough for me to reach the mailbox. Not a problem. He did an immediate U-turn (on two wheels, of course); on the second pass I was able to connect, but only with a glancing blow. After yet another two-wheeled U-turn, in no time we were making another approach. Steve had his head down, focusing his beady little eyes on the target. I was taking dead aim for the little red flag on the side of the mailbox. This time I was leaning way out of the car window with my arm fully extended. I wanted to be sure I could manage the full roundhouse swing necessary to knock the precious little flowery box right into the middle of next week.

Steve was going much faster this time, and also driving much closer to the target than before. To avoid hitting the box with my head or shoulder rather than the hammer, I had to lift my entire torso upwards. This put me off balance. Though I made the long, roundhouse swing I had planned, I missed the box all together. Instead, the completion of the swing brought the hammer all the way around and into the windshield of the Blue Bastard. Fortunately, no harm was done either to the mailbox or my arm, but the same couldn't be said of the windshield.

I suggested to Steve that he should drop me off at my house, go straight home, and explain to Ms. Brasfield what happened to her windshield. Of course, I really wanted to go with him, to tell my role in the story and share the blame. But I felt that Steve and his mother deserved an opportunity to have some good quality time together. Additionally, I wanted to get home ASAP so I could review the devotional we had gone over in Sunday school that morning. As you can see, all of that church activity had a definite impact on me.

Not long after that, Steve and I were to start our junior year at Murrah High School. The school was located on Murrah Drive, which could be entered from Woodrow Wilson Drive at one end or Riverside Drive on the other end. Parents would enter from one direction or the other, drop their kids off, and then continue straight on to exit at the other end.

The night before school began, Steve and I "borrowed" several of the barricades the police department used to block off streets that were under repair. We placed four or five across the entrance to Murrah Drive from Riverside Drive, and then four or five more across Murrah Drive just before the street turned to go in front of the high school. By the time we were finished, cars couldn't get onto Murrah Drive from Riverside, and cars entering from Woodrow Wilson had to make a U-turn to get out.

Steve and I assumed this would be sort of a funny joke. In our vision of things, the police would take down the barricades early the next morning and all would be well. However, we were surprised (well, maybe just a little bit delighted) to find that the police assumed that there was a reason for the roadblocks. Rather than removing the barriers, they enforced them.

This created one "Mell of a hess," as my father used to say. What with the blocked drivers, the U-turns and the general confusion, this wasn't a smooth first day of school.

By the time it was clear that some prankster was to blame, the parents, the school officials, and the police were all pretty ticked off. Now, there is an understatement. For some reason I don't exactly remember, neither Steve nor I ever mentioned our involvement in this little episode until after we had our diplomas in hand two years later.

Steve would eventually become a chemical engineer, and clearly had great aptitude for the work. By senior year, he had learned just enough chemistry to know that if we dropped tin foil in a bottle of hydrochloric acid, it would give off hydrogen gas, which is very explosive. If you remember the *Hindenburg*, you have an example of this. This knowledge led us to concoct a project that required great ingenuity, planning, patience, timing, and sophistication, not to mention Steve's knowledge of chemistry. It also required the theft of some of the necessary components, but we sort of glossed over that part.

We "borrowed" some of the acid from the chemistry lab, took some tin foil from Mrs. Brasfield's kitchen, and brought them to Steve's back yard. I was responsible for gathering a few balloons, some string, a few rags, a box of matches, and a can of kerosene, all of which I did in short order.

Our experiment was now ready. We put the acid in a bottle and then dropped the tin foil into the acid, which immediately began to bubble. We stretched the mouth of the balloon over the top of the bottle. As the hydrogen was produced, it rose into the balloon, causing it to inflate. When the balloon reached sufficient size, we removed it and tied it tightly with the string, which was about fifteen inches long. The other end of the string was tied to a rag dipped in kerosene, which was then lit with a match. Rising, the released balloon was carried off with the wind. As you can see, this was sophisticated planning indeed.

The wind carried the balloons over toward the newly constructed I-55 highway, which ran directly behind Steve's house. After a few tries, we were able to gauge the length of the string to ensure that the fire would reach the balloon just about the time the balloon got to the highway. When the flame reached the balloon, the hydrogen exploded with a loud noise and a puff of black smoke.

The plan went off without a hitch, leaving us delighted with the results. We were busy congratulating ourselves on a job well done when the Mississippi Highway Patrol arrived. Much less impressed than we were with our project, they failed to recognize, much less appreciate, any of the qualities I mentioned earlier and of which we were so proud. If they had been around when Ben Franklin was flying his kite in the thunderstorm, the world might still be using kerosene lanterns.

They began writing out some sort of citation. Then one of them began to laugh, and soon the other followed. Steve and I looked at each other, dumbfounded. Once we felt sure the hilarity wasn't some kind of trick, we began to laugh as well.

In the end, deciding to let us off with their personal warning, the officers tore up the citation. One of them made us promise we wouldn't cause any trouble, and I assured them we wouldn't, if he would let us shoot his gun.

Clarence Lee Lott Jr.

*A*NOTHER ONE OF MY FRIENDS WAS RESPONSIBLE FOR INTRO-
ducing me to the wider world beyond jackson. Knowing me as
you do by now, it will not surprise you that this did not happen without
a few painful moments.

Lee Lott moved to Jackson the summer before his senior year. I
don't remember how we met, only that we became very close friends
in only a short time.

Lee told me on several occasions that his mother did not care for
some of the people he brought around. Especially given my own
somewhat questionable history, I was, and still am, honored that she
was so kind to me. She, Lee's father, and Lee were all very good to me,
and some of my favorite memories revolve around the three of them.

The Lotts had moved to Jackson from Atlanta. Mr. Lott was the
senior executive for Southern Bell in the state of Mississippi. I have no
idea what his title was, but he was the top man in the company for the
entire state. While we lived in a small three-bedroom house on North
State Street, the Lotts lived in a large new house in a much nicer and
newer section of town. Their home was fully carpeted. That was very
unusual, to me at any rate. Even more unusual, they had a phone in

every room with buttons across the bottom indicating multiple lines. I had seen this before, but never in a private home. Mr. and Mrs. Lott were warm, friendly, and gracious. Mr. Lott had a full head of white hair and looked very distinguished, but always seemed pleased to see me and after offering me something to drink would sit down and visit with me. He was obviously very well versed in business, politics, and college football, none of which were ever discussed in my home, and we discussed all of these. Like my great-grandfather Daddy Bogue, he made me feel special by the interest he showed in me. Mrs. Lott seemed less outgoing, but was playful enough to tease us about girls, dating, and the way we dressed, saying that we looked like "Mr. Cool" with our blue suede and white buck shoes.

Lee and I were good friends during our senior year. Not long after we graduated from Murrah High, his family invited me to go with them for some sort of business meeting that his father was attending on the Mississippi Gulf Coast. Lee and I had our own room. We would call room service as soon as we awakened—usually around 1:30 p.m. or so—for a nutritious breakfast of hamburgers, fries, and Coca-Colas. Left to our own devices, we would sit in the sun, eat at the hotel restaurant, and go to the nightclubs that were within walking distance and that did not require IDs.

To make things even better, a friend of Lee's father named W. O. McDowell called and told us that he had managed to rent a pickup truck for our use. Mr. McDowell was one of Mr. Lott's top people in the telephone company. He took us down to the parking lot. Pointing to a broken-down truck with torn upholstery and a damaged front fender, he apologized and said it was the best he could do. We were absolutely thrilled. Assuring him that it was perfect and thanking him profusely, we anxiously ran toward it. Just as we were about to open the door, we heard Mr. McDowell yell, "Just for kicks, why don't you try the keys in that pretty little blue convertible next to the pickup!"

Unbelievable! Lee and I had the time of our lives in that beautiful car, at least until we wrecked it. But why go into that minor little detail?

Not too long after that, Lee's father asked me if I would like to go dove hunting. I would be welcome, he said, as long as I did not mind eating beans out of a can and sleeping on the ground. I told him that I certainly didn't mind, but that I didn't own a shotgun and had never even fired one. Assuring me that he had an extra gun, Mr. Lott said that he would have someone pick me up and teach me how to use it on the way to the hunt.

The morning of the hunt, three gentlemen from Southern Bell Telephone Company arrived at my house. One of the men was Mr. McDowell, who thankfully seemed to have forgotten about the convertible mishap. He sat on the back seat with another gentleman and me.

As promised, they gave me a complete course in bird hunting on the way to the delta. They told me how to lead the birds as they flew across my path, coming toward me and flying away from me. They even explained how to avoid hitting the other hunters with buckshot. I bet that the friend on the receiving end of some of Vice President Cheney's buckshot in 2006 wished Mr. Cheney had been in that car for some of this excellent instruction.

When we arrived at the lodge where the hunt was held, we were greeted with a catered lunch of fried chicken or steak. I looked hard, but I wasn't able to find the beans Mr. Lott had warned me about. About 3 p.m. I was in the field hunting just like I knew what I was doing. Even though it was my first time to ever fire a shotgun, I shot nineteen birds that afternoon. But I guess I should not have admitted that, since the limit was ten.

I was standing next to Mr. Lott when a man called out to him from the bed of a pickup truck. "Clarence, come over here!"

"Leave me alone, Johnson. I'm busy killing birds!" Mr. Lott yelled back.

When Mr. Johnson insisted, Mr. Lott told me to come along and see what the problem was. When we arrived, Mr. Johnson took some folding chairs off of the truck for us and served us chilled pink Champagne. I immediately decided I could get used to "roughing it, Lott style" without too much trouble. Like the beans from a can, the sleeping bag Mr. Lott had promised was also missing—we were put up in a hotel. When dinner time came, Lee and I were given directions to the country club. The grown men didn't join us for our meal. No doubt they went to church or Bible study. I never did figure out why they would need all those decks of cards to go to Bible study. Maybe it was a Methodist thing.

Though Lee and I were naturally disappointed to miss out on the Bible study with the men, we had a wonderful time at the country club and felt like a couple of big shots. After dinner we went and sat at the bar, where a delightful gentleman waited on us all evening. I think he must have known 10,000 jokes, at least one of which was clean. However, he only managed to tell us a couple of hundred, which was probably why he forgot to tell us the clean one.

Sitting at the country club bar in my coat and tie and acting like a big shot, I felt it was appropriate to order a drink. I knew nothing about how to do so. My father had an occasional beer, but no one I knew drank liquor. Deciding to let the movies be my guide, I said, "I'll have a martini."

A few minutes later, the bartender placed the drink in front of me. It had to be the worst tasting thing I had ever put in my mouth. Like castor oil, it was a liquid I couldn't believe anyone would drink voluntarily. I worked at it for a long time, taking tiny little sips but making very little progress.

I had to do something. "Refresh my memory," I whispered to the bartender in my most mature and debonair tone. "Exactly what is in a martini?"

"Gin and vermouth," he answered with a slight grin on his kind face.

Though I knew so little about liquor, I did know what gin was. I figured vermouth was probably a mixer, something like ginger ale. I asked if the bartender would put some more vermouth in my drink, which he gladly did.

I felt relieved. I had handled a tricky situation without Lee so much as guessing how totally unsophisticated I was. Tipping my glass to my friend and the bartender, I took a rather large sip—actually, more of a small gulp.

There was an instant fire in my esophagus. My eyes began to water. They probably even crossed as I tried desperately to suppress the urge to vomit or do something even worse. As casually as possible I excused myself, strolled into the men's room and regrouped.

When I returned, Lee was laughing uncontrollably as the punch line of the most recent joke was finished. My drink still sat on the bar waiting. For the next few minutes I took the most minuscule sips possible. Finally, the bartender put his elbow on the bar and leaned toward me, smiling. "Do you want me to bring you something you can actually drink?" he whispered.

"Perhaps that would be best," I said. He returned with a Tom Collins, which I suspect had little, if any, alcohol in it. It tasted like lemonade compared to the martini.

As these stories suggest, the Lott family lived a far more privileged life than my own. Talking to Lee, you would never have known this. He was warm and friendly to everyone, and had a strong character. Knowing his parents, it was easy to see where these good qualities came from.

In addition to introducing me to luxuries such as champagne and room service, Mr. Lott taught me some valuable lessons. He believed that what made America great was our free enterprise system, which gave every individual with sufficient will and determination the freedom to rise.

Successful as he himself was, he wasn't too busy to talk about such things to a young man. He told me how he had started at the bottom and worked his way up in the company. He told that if I was willing to work hard and treated people with respect, I could accomplish whatever it was that I wanted to do. He said he admired people like my father who worked hard and stood behind their work. He said, as did my father, to always "let your word be your bond," "Say what you mean and mean what you say."

I can't pretend that I didn't enjoy having the Lotts put me up in a hotel, bring me to a dove hunt, or send me to a country club to eat. Those were wonderful experiences for me. But it was the Lotts themselves, and not the glamorous settings, that were so delightful. I can honestly say that if they had been present, sleeping on the ground and eating baked beans out of a can would have been just fine.

Working Toward College

*W*HEN I WAS A KID MY TOP TEETH STUCK ALMOST STRAIGHT out. This would have been handy had I needed to eat an apple through a picket fence, but it wasn't useful for much else. Fortunately this problem was corrected by my orthodontist, Dr. Curtis Russ, whom I saw every two weeks for four years. I was fascinated by the whole process. I am sure I must have driven Dr. Russ to near insanity with my constant questions; I don't think he ever put an instrument in my mouth without having explained in detail exactly what it was supposed to do. I decided I wanted to become an orthodontist and, later, that I wanted to go to Ole Miss as a pre-dental student. However, times were hard financially for my parents and I wasn't sure they could afford it.

A friend of my mother's named Quida Howard found out about a lady in Memphis that wanted to give a student interested in medicine a scholarship to go to Southwestern, which later became the Rhodes College. The scholarship was endowed in honor of the lady's uncle, a fellow named Faulkner who was a colonel in the Civil War. Mrs. Howard arranged for me to visit Southwestern and interview for the scholarship. I interviewed first with the donor's banker and later with the donor herself. The good news was that I was awarded the scholarship. The bad news was that I did not want to go to Southwestern. It was certainly an excellent school, but it felt rather stuffy. For example, it required students to march into the dining room for dinner at 6:00 p.m. sharp, wearing a coat and tie. That was way too regimented for my taste.

I told my parents I wanted to turn down the scholarship. I would go to Millsaps College, which was right in Jackson, and live at home to save money. But when I communicated my decision to the scholarship's banker, he assured me that the scholarship was mine no matter what school I wished to attend.

With the funds my parents could provide, my own savings, and the scholarship, I would be able to enter the pre-dental program at Ole Miss. All I needed to do was earn and save some money in the summers. Always supportive of me, Mr. Lott got me a job working for Divinney Construction Company the summer after I graduated from high school. Mr. Divinney's company did a lot of work for the telephone company. As for Mr. Divinney himself, I can only say that he was a man of few words. He was pleasant, but always brisk and businesslike. I was told that he was a self-made man and worked for everything he had, and had done extremely well. I was also told that he had once shot his favorite hunting dog for running through a covey of quails. While that story was probably untrue, it sure made the people working for him think twice about goofing off.

I was told that I would be doing construction work. It worried me to think that I might end up with my hands wrapped around a post hole digger, digging holes for telephone poles. But on my first day on the job, I was told to go down to an old dairy barn on "Mr. D's" property. About the size of a three-car garage and without windows, it had doors at either end and a concrete floor. Two concrete structures, like low walls, ran from one end of the building to the other. Maybe they were meant to keep cows separated while they were being milked, but

I'm not really sure. I was a city boy and city boys don't "know nuthin bout" milking.

As I looked around the barn, the foreman came up to me, introducing himself and another fellow. The fellow was named Tom but the foreman's name escapes me now. Pointing to a jackhammer in the corner of the room, he stated that Tom and I would be using it to tear all the concrete out of the barn floor.

He then carefully demonstrated the use of the jackhammer, which weighed about seventy pounds. He said we were to place the end of the jackhammer where we wanted it and then to compress the lever on the side of the handle and hang on tightly as the action started. The foreman emphasized that we had to be very careful to not let our feet get in the way of the end of the jackhammer.

"Yeah, I bet that would give you a bad stubbed toe for sure," I said sarcastically.

He looked at me with shock. "You stupid son of a bitch, if that thing lands on your toe it will tear your damned foot clean off," he said with obvious disgust.

Once again, I learned what it was like to make a sarcastic comment to someone who doesn't understand your sarcasm. The result is always the same. They either think that you're an idiot or that you're just plain stupid. Well, maybe I shouldn't say that I learned this lesson, because the same thing continues to happen to me all the time. Someday maybe I'll learn not to be sarcastic. Okay, maybe not. This seems to be part of my sense of humor. I guess I'm stuck with it.

Fortunately, there was only one jackhammer, so Tom and I had to alternate using it. This worked out quite well to begin with, since neither one of us could go more than fifteen minutes before virtually collapsing in the corner. It felt like the jackhammer was going to shake the teeth out of your head. Also, the jackhammer that had weighed 70 pounds at 7 a.m. weighed at least 170 pounds by 10:30. By 3 p.m. I think the darned thing weighed closer to 350 pounds, possibly more.

By the end of the first day, Tom and I were both totally exhausted and drenched in sweat. We were so tired we could hardly move. Meanwhile, the dust from the torn-up concrete had settled on our skin and in our hair, where it combined with our sweat to turn back into concrete. This made me the truly hardheaded person I had always been accused of being. Our fingers were sore, swollen and locked into the claw position we had used to hang on to the jackhammer handles. I don't know about Tom, but not being able to get my hands out of the claw position made it very difficult for me to drive home. When I got there, all I could do was fall across the bed. I don't think I moved until the following morning, when I got in the shower as hot as I could stand. I let it run until it turned cold, trying to dilute the concrete enough to wash it off of my body and out of my hair.

But the body can acclimate to most anything, especially when that body is young. Within a couple of days, Tom and I could easily run the jackhammer all day. In fact, we could actually run it with one hand while sipping a Coca-Cola held in the other hand.

As you know, I had had several misadventures with paint in my younger years. Even though I eventually learned to paint quite well and ended up doing quite a bit of painting, I never liked it. Just about the time Tom and I were finishing up with the dairy barn, Mr. D. came in to look over our work. Out of the blue he asked if I could paint. I said, ""Yes, sir." That was a big mistake. I should have said, "No sir, never was any good at painting and always make a terrible mess." However, being intimidated by Mr. D. and not able to think quickly enough to tell that little fib, I ended up painting most of the inside of the Divinneys' house. That was a royal pain. The house had a lot of fancy molding as well as very expensive carpet. To make matters worse, Mr. D's picky wife was constantly looking over my shoulder. By the time I finished the painting job, I was almost nostalgic for the jackhammer.

I also helped the roofers put a roof on Mr. D's house that summer. We worked in the hot August sun, which made the already backbreaking work even more miserable. Even though I wore two pairs of socks and work boots with thick soles, I still had blisters on the bottom of my feet by the end of the day. We split up our shift so that we would work from 5:30 to 9:30 in the morning and then again from 4:30 to 8:30 in the evening. Even so, it was still hotter than the hinges of Hades. The shingles came in bundles that were not only heavy, but very cumbersome to carry up the ladder. The nice roofers let me carry all of the bundles up to the roof. Daddy said that all I had to do was carry the shingles up the ladder and that the guys up on the roof did all the work. He was joking but I can't say I found the joke very funny.

A man named Mr. Frith was the carpenter who did most of the work on Mr. D.'s house, overseeing the two other men doing carpentry work. Mr. Frith, an excellent carpenter and a very interesting gentleman, took a genuine interest in me. He seemed fascinated that I planned to go to dental school and always called me "Doc." He was a hard worker and a perfectionist who said that I should always do what I promised and never cut corners. He gave me other sage advice about life in general, pointing out that no matter how important a person becomes in life, his poo-poo will always stink. He might not have phrased it exactly that way, but that was the gist of the message.

Mr. Frith also gave me advice about how to handle my wife when I married. "Doc," he would say, "don't ever mistreat any lady. But you gotta let 'em know right off who's the boss!" He illustrated this admonition with a story. When he was first married, he had come home from work for three days straight only to find his bride down the street at Mama's house. Every night, it was over an hour before she came home to cook dinner. On the third day he went to Mama's house and called his bride outside. He told her in front of her mother that he got home every afternoon at 3:30 p.m. He expected her to be there and to have dinner on the table at 4:30 sharp. If she had a problem with that, he told his wife, she could move back in with Mama.

Mr. Frith said that things had run smoothly after that. Ever since, his dinner had been on the table at 4:30 on the dot. Interestingly, I have been married twice and the Frith approach did not to work with either of my wives. Guess I should have paid better attention. I must have missed a step in there somewhere.

Mr. Frith once asked me if I liked dove. I told him that indeed I did. Saying that he was going dove hunting, he promised to bring me all the dove I could eat the following Monday.

"Don't you like dove?" I asked him.

"I would never eat a dove! They are the birds of peace," he answered. I thought it fascinating that he was willing to blow the poor birds right out of the sky but wouldn't eat them. It certainly worked well for me, however. He brought about fifteen dove the following Monday, and my family enjoyed them immensely.

It was a good summer, all in all. I managed to save a few bucks to put toward college and I realized that if the college and doctoring thing did not work out, I could always make a living running a jackhammer, roofing, and painting. Having some college money in the bank and this solid backup plan gave me the peace of mind I needed. *Ole Miss,* I thought at the end of the summer, *here I come.*

Freshman Year

*N*OW THAT YOU HAVE BECOME FAMILIAR WITH MY MANY childhood mishaps, you may be surprised to see that I not only lived to adulthood but also got into college. Had they read this book, perhaps Ole Miss would have made a different decision on my application. However, they accepted me for matriculation in the fall of 1958. I duly prepared myself for life as a college freshman in the thriving metropolis of Oxford, Mississippi, campus location, 180 miles north of Jackson.

Like most freshmen, I was a little anxious as my first year of college approached. I had been to Ole Miss several times during my junior and senior years and had also visited other colleges and universities as well. The fact that my friend Steve Brasfield was to be my college roommate was also reassuring. All of that made the transition more comfortable, but when the time came to leave home I was still both excited and a little unnerved.

I was able to get everything I took with me to Ole Miss in the trunk of my father's car. I brought every item that I thought would be necessary. I took clothes, a dictionary, a thesaurus, a three-ring binder in case I decided to take notes, and a small AM radio. What else could I possibly need? Then I realized that all the cool dudes on campus had a trench coat, so I rushed out to get one. Unfortunately, it seemed that all of the other freshmen must have had the same idea, as there were very few trench coats left. The only one I could find was a size 44, so I bought it. Since I was a size 37 it looked more like I was wearing a tent from Army Surplus than a raincoat. But then, I'm getting ahead of myself.

We arrived on the campus just before noon on an August morning. Incoming cars carrying freshman were instructed to stop at a makeshift barbershop on the lawn in front of a building just inside the campus. Once there, I was ordered to sit while an upperclassman shaved my head and gave me my Ole Miss beanie. I was commanded to wear the beanie at all times and told that there would be hell to pay if I lost it or allowed it to be snatched off of my head. This would be especially problematic if said beanie was snatched by anyone from Mississippi Damn State. Looking around me, I realized that the upperclassmen didn't actually shave your head or even give you a buzz cut. They just cut your hair so short and ragged looking that the only logical thing to do was to go to the barbershop and have your remaining hair removed with the barber clippers.

Wearing my new beanie, I went with my family up the hill toward the men's dorms. Girls were not permitted in this area, but mothers were allowed, at least on this particular day. We stopped at Baxter Dormitory, a rather plain and unimpressive three-story brick building. We made our way up the concrete stairs to the second floor and found the room that Steve and I would occupy. Steve was sitting there waiting on us. Having been there a good twenty minutes, he was already settled in. He had hung a few of his clothes in the closet and thrown the rest of them on his half of the closet floor. That arrangement seemed reasonable to me, and I looked forward to doing the same once my mother left.

Baxter Dorm had a long hall that ran all the way through the second floor and a single wall telephone in the middle. The rooms were probably 12 x 12 feet square with two windows, one closet, two single beds, two metal desks, and two metal chairs. Each room had its own sink, but at each end of the hall there was a bathroom with open showers and four toilet stalls. To say that the place was Spartan is an understatement. I always suspected that cells at the state prison served as the model for our room design and furnishings. The windows had no shades and the closets and toilet stalls had no doors. All the floors were concrete, lacking rugs or even linoleum. Clearly, Ole Miss knew something about the habits of boys our age. The entire dormitory looked as if it had been designed to be hosed down from time to time without damaging a thing.

It took only a short time to unload my meager belongings into the small room. With this done, my parents soon left. Giving me a big hug, my mother got somewhat emotional. Actually, we all were, but Daddy and I weren't about to show it. We started to shake hands like two tough guys. At the last minute, he grabbed me for a hug, which felt much better than the tough guy approach had. Daddy stood there for a while trying to think of some reason to stay longer, but finally it was time for them to go. Mother was tearful as they drove off and Daddy and I weren't far from it. When they got in the car and slowly drove away, a part of me went with them. I knew just how lucky I was to have both of them in my life and was taken aback to think that now I would have to learn to make my way without them.

Steve and I threw ourselves into the flurry of activities that took place in the few days before school actually started. The events I remember best were the afternoon and evening fraternity rush parties. The frats also did "drop-bys," when members of a given fraternity would visit your room to tell you all the wonderful things about their particular group. The tobacco companies handed out packs of four cigarettes of their respective brands to the fraternities, which would give them to freshmen going through rush. In those days, just about everyone smoked, and these "smokers" were where many of us picked up the ridiculous habit.

After the last rush party I put Sigma Chi as my first and only choice. If they had not selected me I would have been totally out of luck, but to my delight they did.

Just before school started, we had to undergo some academic testing, which determined our placement in freshman English classes. Having made A's in English throughout high school, I wasn't concerned about this. To my surprise, my new brothers explained that it was very much to my advantage to do *poorly* on these entrance tests. Those who got low scores were placed amid others with similarly low skill levels; since English classes were graded on a curve, getting good grades would be much easier in a class of poor students than in a class of excellent ones.

Ignoring idealistic notions about actual learning, I took this advice to heart. During the English placement test I happily labeled nouns as adverbs, pronouns as prepositions, and adjectives as conjunctions. It worked like a charm. On my first day in English, I discovered two girls from Venezuela who barely spoke the language and three football players who were taking English 101 for the second or third time. I am not sure why, but this course was taught by a small lady professor who was an outstanding teacher and chain-smoked Chesterfields. It was probably the easiest A I ever made.

One of our first assignments was to write an outline about making something. I went out on a limb and wrote about making a bird house. I don't remember what all I said, except that it was all very tongue in cheek. The plans included installing functional roll-away newspaper carpet, consulting the birds about length of runways, and adding an adjoining house in the back for the nagging mother-in-law. On the way to class that morning I became very nervous about turning this effort in. Instead, the professor loved it, read it in class, and gave me an A-plus, telling me that she expected great things out of me. We then had to write a couple of short stories. Despite my teacher's high expectations I felt totally inadequate to do so. I talked my fellow student Charles Alexander from high school into helping me. Well, to be honest, he didn't "help me," he just wrote them for me. His stories were good for A's also.

I made the honor roll first semester, and I was asked to join the school's honors program. When I met with the program director, who was also my English professor, I mentioned that I planned to go to college for only the three years to get the necessary requirements for medical school. She was clearly appalled at this plan. In addition to telling me that it would make me ineligible for the honors program, I remember her looking me straight in the eye and saying, "You don't know where the f@#* you are going, so why are you in such a rush to get there?"

I probably looked at her with my mouth wide open. In 1958, people in general, and certainly ladies in particular, did not use the F-word, especially in mixed company. I'm sorry to say that I did not heed her advice. But I have never forgotten it, and long ago realized that she was absolutely correct. Going to college for just three years gave me the bare essentials to get into medical school, but little else. Missing so much history, literature, classical and social studies and all the rest was a real loss.

Steve and I studied hard. That was sometimes hard to do in a dormitory filled with boys with only a few hours of class a day and no four-hour labs. I remember several big party weekends when we checked into a cheap motel for the weekend so we could study. But we also spent an inordinate amount of time playing wild and bizarre tricks on each other. I remember standing at the sink shaving early one morning, half asleep after studying most of the night. All of a sudden, there was a loud banging on the window. Since we lived on the second floor and nothing could reach our window except a giraffe or maybe a dinosaur—neither of which I had ever seen on the Ole Miss campus—the noise startled the daylights out of me. I pulled our makeshift curtains aside to find that Steve had scaled the wall. "I gotcha!" he said with a huge grin. And so he had. But I think he may have felt less triumphant when he found a large portion of chocolate pudding between his sheets when he crawled into bed that night.

By the end of the year, we were absolutely exhausted. As many college freshmen can tell you, balancing studying, practical jokes, and fraternity parties is a tiring task. Sick of studying, we just wanted to get away from it all. Steve suggested we go to his father's cabin on a lake outside of Vicksburg. We could use the their fishing boat, which had a very small motor, take it up the Yazoo River, camp out, catch so many fish we'd get sick of eating them, and just relax. We called John Ricks, a classmate from Murrah, who was a freshman in pre-med at Vanderbilt. As tired of studying as we were, he readily agreed to join us, saying, "Count me in."

In addition to being sick of studying, Steve, John, and I were sick of being on a schedule. We decided that we would take this trip with no planning whatsoever. According to plan, we left Jackson en route to Vicksburg with absolutely no plans at all. Just before arriving at the lake, we did decide that we would stop and pick up a few things for the night. We each purchased a case of beef stew and a case of beer. What else could we need?

We got to the lake around 6 p.m. Rather than stay at the cabin that night, we loaded up the boat and headed out. Steve had forgotten to mention one little obstacle to going up the Yazoo: a small dam between the lake and the river. It took us more than an hour and several beers to get the boat over the dam. Then we were off. The weather was perfect, and the beer was cold. All was well.

As we journeyed up the river, we began to notice that it was starting to get dark. This should not sound surprising, but for some reason it was. Maybe the beers were having some effect. Within no time it was pitch black. There was no moon, and we had only one small flashlight. We searched the shore for any spot with sufficient clearing to set up camp. The only such place that we could find was up a small bluff, about six to eight feet above the water. On the way up to it, I took a step onto what I thought was the bank. Instead, I was stepping into the river. I went in well over my head. John and Steve thought this was hilarious, but for some reason, I wasn't amused.

By the time we finally got to the top of the landing, we were ravenous. It was too dark to see much of anything, much less start a campfire. Then we realized that we did not even have a can opener. This no-planning thing was really working out well. We had to open the cans of beef stew with a knife and eat the stew straight from the can. I can remember waking up in the middle of the night thinking that I would gladly sell my soul for an Alka-Seltzer.

While the beef stew and cold beer had tasted great the night before, the next morning we found a breakfast of cold beef stew and warm beer to be somewhat lacking. And lunch wasn't any better. Either the river didn't have the plentiful supply of fish Steve had promised or we were too inept to catch them. In the three days that we were on the river, we caught exactly one small fish.

Just in case we encountered any trouble, Steve had brought a .22 rifle and I had brought my father's German Luger, which, as far as I knew, had never been fired since the end of World War II. (As you may recall, one of the 9 mm bullets had been fired, but the gun itself had not.) Luckily, we did not need the weapons. We would have been in a real mess if we had. All three of us tried multiple times to hit a beer can from ten feet away with the German Luger, but the can remained unscathed.

All in all, it was a trip we would never forget. Most memorable of all was our unanimous decision that our next trip would be well planned and thoroughly thought out, and our equally unanimous realization that maybe school and studying weren't as bad as we'd thought.

Furniture, Friends,
and Fondren Pink Layer Cakes

*L*EAVING HOME TO GO TO OLE MISS, I LEFT MY FAMILY AND the traditions of the Big House behind. But as you have already learned, I didn't entirely shed the "dickens" that I'd been full of in childhood. Nor did I lose my Fondren identity.

There were a lot of things that set the Fondrens apart from everybody else. Not just things such as family values, sayings, and habits. Really important things like birthday cakes as well. Fondren tradition dictated that our family's birthday cakes were different from all others. First of all, a Fondren birthday cake was a real honest-to-goodness "scratch" cake. No box cakes here! In the family's estimation, any lady who would make a birthday cake out of a box probably smoked cigars, wore combat boots, and made chocolate pies with instant pudding mix.

Secondly, Fondren birthday cakes always had a pink center. Don't ask me why. They just did. The pink center was created by putting in a few drops of red food coloring in the middle layer. I may not know how this got started, but I can tell you that when you cut into your birthday cake and spied that pink center, you knew you were special. You knew you were a Fondren, or at least a close friend of a Fondren, and either one of those was pretty darn good.

I never thought about any of that until my freshman year in college, which was the first time I had ever been away from home on my birthday. Mama promised that she would mail me a birthday cake. Sure enough, the package from home arrived on the exact date of my birthday. I grabbed the package, carried it to the fraternity house, and told everyone exactly what to expect from what was inside, pink center and all.

I removed the tape, paper, and string and opened the box somewhat gingerly. Then four layers of tin foil and two layers of plastic wrap had to be carefully removed. Finally, there was my birthday cake, just a little bit the worse for wear, but looking pretty darn good.

I took a big knife out of the kitchen and cut into it. "See, I told you..." But I'd been wrong. All of the layers, even the middle one, were just plain ordinary white.

Oh my gosh, I thought. *What happened?* Where's my pink center? Did Mama have a little stroke? Doesn't she love me anymore? Maybe she's still upset because I once shot all the paint off her stove. Maybe she found out I had a date with that sorority girl who smoked those funny little cigarettes and said bad words. Maybe this is her way of telling me I was adopted and never really a Fondren after all.

I invested a not inconsiderable amount of change into a pay phone call to confront Mama about this obvious breach of family values. She said she was afraid that if she put a pink layer in my cake everyone at Ole Miss would laugh and think I was some kind of sissy. I told her that I didn't care what the heck that bunch of idiots thought. From now on, I wanted my Fondren pink layer.

As always, my mother came through. A few days later, I received another cake in the mail. This time, *all* of the layers were pink.

As I've said, Steve Brasfield and I were roommates during our freshman year. The following year, Steve and our Murrah classmate,

Warren Todd, who was also in the school of engineering, decided to room together, so Lee Lott and I paired up.

To be perfectly honest, I think mine and Lee's deciding to room together had less to do with our friendship than the fact we were both such slobs that no one else would room with either of us. I remember Lee's father dropping in on us unexpectedly one afternoon. He looked a bit queasy as he proclaimed to Mrs. Lott that the only way our room could have been a bigger mess was for it to have been a bigger room.

During his freshman year, Lee had had a little too much fun. In fact, I think that even if he had doubled his GPA, he still wouldn't have passed. When I asked Lee what his father's response to his grades had been, he said that his father had told him he had one semester to screw up, and he had just had it. If he turned in another performance of this nature, Mr. Lott warned, Lee would find himself digging holes for telephone poles for Southern Bell. That, in turn, would mean an instant invitation to the U. S. Army—the Vietnam War was ongoing at that time and the draft was in force. Mr. Lott gave me firm instructions to monitor Lee's study habits. But Lee knew his father meant what he said, and had no further problems with his grades.

I learned a lot from Lee that year and enjoyed being his roommate. He was warm and friendly to everyone—no one would ever have known of his father's prominent position or his family's wealth from talking to him. I very much admired this. Lee had a strong character; knowing his parents, it was easy to see where this came from.

Steve Brasfield and I were in different schools, different fraternities, and lived in different rooms our sophomore year. The separation continued during our junior years, when we both lived in our respective fraternity houses. Despite not seeing much of each other during that time, our antics continued.

Our most memorable prank was inspired by the contrasting styles of our fraternity houses. The Sigma Chi house, where I lived, was of a very modern design and had sleek Danish-style furniture. Members of other fraternities said it looked more like a Phillips 66 service station than a fraternity house. Steve lived in the Phi Delta Theta house. It was a large, white, two-story Colonial complete with a big porch and white columns. Its traditional look continued in its interior, which was decorated with heavy, overstuffed couches and large chairs.

Steve and I bumped into each other one night at the Sigma Chi house after a party. We talked late into the night, becoming more and more "under the weather." I feel sure that we solved most of the world's problems with great insight that night. As an example, I remember commenting, "The drunker we sit here, the longer we get." Sometime during the evening, we were joined by another fine Sigma Chi, who by then was getting "pretty long" himself. I don't want to mention his name, but his initials were Thad Rudd from Indiana.

It was about 4 a.m. when we had a truly brilliant idea. Given the different styles of our respective fraternity houses, we decided that exchanging their furniture would be an educational cultural exchange for both—a kind of Winter Term Abroad, if you will. The houses were not side-by-side; in fact, the Phi Delta Theta house was up a slight hill and there was another fraternity house between it and the Sigma Chi house. But no matter. Do minor inconveniences really count when greater community understanding is at stake?

With energy inconceivable to anyone older or less drunk, we moved all of the Sigma Chi furniture, pictures, trophies, lamps, and everything else that wasn't nailed down to Phi Delta Theta House and vice versa. We did a masterful job (at least through our somewhat inebriated eyes) of re-arranging the furniture, plugging in the lamps, hanging the pictures, and placing trophies we had moved in the wall cabinets. Even more remarkably, we managed not to be detected. Then, with an oath of secrecy, we went home and went to bed. I think it was around 5:30 a.m., and just starting to get light.

Later that morning, I was awakened by an uproar. I remember one fraternity brother standing in my room screaming that there was nothing but pictures of *#!** Phi Deltas on our walls and *&%$# Phi Delta trophies on all of our shelves. Others were running around shouting urgently about the need to call the Mississippi National Guard, a lawyer, and the fraternity council, not necessarily in that order.

The three of us watched with interest through bloodshot eyes as the pledges of both fraternity houses worked hard for several hours undoing what three drunks had done in the dark of night in a much shorter period of time. It was worth all of our effort just to observe the number of people in both houses who got into a complete uproar over their determination to find the culprits. I don't think anyone even vaguely considered that it had been an inside job involving brothers of both houses. I did not tell anyone for many years, and I don't think the others did either.

Steve Brasfield and I remained good friends through it all. Quite simply, no one was more fun to be with than Steve. Looking back at our antics with what little wisdom I have gained over the years, I'm just glad that we never ended up downtown after one of our "harmless" little pranks, holding up a set of numbers over our chest for a police lineup and perhaps changing our futures forever.

Changes at the Big House

ESPITE ALL EXPECTATIONS THAT I WOULD ACCIDENTALLY blow myself to smithereens and never see the age of twenty, I managed not only to survive my many boyish pranks but even to impress enough folks that I was admitted to the freshman class of Ole Miss for the 1958-59 school year. Though of course I continued to return home after I went to college, in some ways my journey to Ole Miss marked the end of my childhood. Not only was I going off to live more or less independently, I was entering a new life that did not have Jackson as its center. It was a big change.

Naturally, the Fondren family and the Big House were changing along with me. As I've mentioned, Grandaddy died in 1944. Gran followed him to Heaven in 1947. Aunt May, who never married, lived in the Big House from the time she was born until the day it was sold.

My family moved in with her shortly after Gran died. But by 1952 it was obvious that such a large house was too impractical and expensive for only three adults and four children to live in. The Big House property was sold in 1953.

My family moved into a three-bedroom house about twenty blocks further down North State Street. Aunt May moved in with Aunt Ella, a widow by then, to live in a duplex on Fondren Place directly behind the Big House.

The Old Testament used the term "begat" to refer to procreation or the generation of offspring. Since the Fondren family always seemed to be very efficient at "begetting," the family had expanded to well over forty members by this time. Since the Big House was gone, no one had a home large enough for a group of this size.

Refusing to be denied the warmth and love of these family gatherings, Aunt May built a screened porch along the back of Aunt Ella's free-standing garage. This elongated structure with a concrete floor was approximately sixteen feet long and less than eight feet wide—just wide enough to fit a single serving table. On Sundays and holidays, the family loaded this table with covered dishes. We would circle around the table, piling our plates as full as possible, and then convene in the yard for a picnic-style lunch. Sometimes hamburgers would be cooked on the grill and served with watermelon, homemade ice cream and, of course, sweet tea.

Because it was screened rather than closed in, it was only usable in the warmer months. So the little porch behind the garage became affectionately know as the Summer House.

The Fondren gatherings continued through the 1950s. By then the family had begat itself to an even larger size, and many of its members had dispersed to other parts of the state and country. The gatherings occurred less and less frequently, and eventually stopped altogether.

After its sale, the Big House was eventually torn down, and an insurance company building was erected on the site. It was strange to see that place of such warmth replaced by a site of cold, unfeeling commerce.

But at the risk of sounding corny, I guess you could say that the Big House itself was a kind of insurance operation.

It insured that all of the children raised in or around it would know what it felt like to be deeply loved, lovingly teased, unquestioningly accepted and, when necessary, justly shown the error of their ways.

It insured that we would grow up with lives full of warmth—with relatives that weren't just family but also friends, and friends that were as enduring as family.

It insured that we would have wonderful role models, mentors, and teachers—folks with clear values as well as colorful personalities.

It insured that we would have plenty of stories to tell and traditions to share with our kids, and their kids, and their kids' kids beyond that.

I feel lucky to have had the actual Big House in my life for so long. But the profound meaning the place had, and has, for me never lay in its physical structure. The essence of the Big House wasn't a big house. It was a big family, with a big heart.

And luckily, that's something that can be carried anywhere, no matter how much the world changes.

Afterword I:

My Father, Inventor and Entrepreneur

*I*N HIS LATER LIFE, MY FATHER WENT ON TO BECOME AN INTER-nationally appreciated inventor and businessman. Many of his most notable accomplishments occurred beyond the timeframe covered in his story, but I don't want to close the book without honoring his achievements.

Though they didn't gain him money or recognition until much later, Daddy's flair for both handwork and invention started in his childhood. His mother was a sweet person who had a heart condition, and there-fore spent most of her adult life as a shut-in and a "cardiac cripple." Granddaddy Keeton was a bookkeeper for a lumber company. In an attempt to keep Daddy out of his mother's way, Granddaddy would bring home truckloads of wood scraps from the lumber company and dump them in the backyard. Giving my father a few tools and some nails, he instructed him to "make things" out in the yard, and to stay out of his mother's way. Not much of a woodworker himself, Grand-daddy did not give Daddy much if any instruction about how to use the tools or what the heck to make. But the time spent with wood and the freedom to experiment stood Daddy in good stead. Over the years he became a proficient woodworker, using his skills not only to create things for our house but in his professional work.

My father's lack of formal education was a lifelong frustration to him. I remember his reading the want ads over and over, looking for ways to make a living. He told me many times how hard it was for someone with no education to find work. This made an indelible impression on me. I did not yet know what I was going to do or be, but I promised myself that I would never be at the mercy of finding a job in the want ads.

When they were first married, my parents lived in an apartment at the Big House. Just off of the kitchen, it consisted of one bedroom with an outside entrance and the only bathroom on the first floor of the Big House. With children coming, Daddy knew he was going to have to make more money if he was going to be able to survive. He told Granddaddy Fondren that while he had never made a fireplace mantel, he had studied them closely. He was sure that he could easily make and sell them if he just had somewhere to work. After pondering for a while, Granddaddy found a man who had a small building he didn't need and paid to have it moved to the back yard of the Big House. This workshop was very small. If Daddy needed to turn the mantel he was working on, he had to take it outside. Despite such challenges, he not only made beautiful mantels but made a nice profit off from them, too.

After my parents had lived in the Big House apartment for five years, Granddaddy Fondren gave them a lot on Mitchell Avenue. Daddy borrowed three thousand dollars to build a small two-bedroom house with a one-car garage on the property. At that time, my family did not own a car and had no intention of buying one. The garage was built to provide Daddy with a workshop. Though it was small, it seemed enormous compared to his former workshop at the Big House. He was thrilled with it. After supper each evening, he would go straight to his new shop and work until 11: 30, making mantels and anything else he could sell for extra cash.

Once they were settled in their new house, Daddy told Mama that he wanted to make something really special for her. What did she want, more than anything else? After thinking for a while she said that she would love to have a china cabinet, but the dining room was simply too small for one. Instead, she wanted a pair of china cabinets that would fit in the corners, taking up much less space.

Daddy scratched his head at that. He didn't know about that idea, he said, as he had never seen a corner china cabinet. "But if that's what you want, that's what you will get!" he added with a big grin on his face. The corner cabinets he built were beautiful, and my parents moved them to each of their new homes over the next 50 years.

Daddy often took on difficult woodworking tasks. I remember him coming back from the workshop saying that what he had undertaken was impossible—it simply couldn't be done. With that he would go straight to bed, where he would toss and turn all night in frustration. He would get up the next morning and go to work, but the unfinished project stayed in the back of his mind. After work he would come home and look at Mama with a grin on his face. "Well, I can't believe it, but I finally figured it out. Now I'm going go out there and do it," he would say, and indeed he would.

As I've mentioned in some of this book's chapters, he never took any shortcuts. As far as he was concerned, there was only one way to do things, and that was the right way. All of his life, the family teased him about this, joking that anything and everything he made was strong enough for elephants to dance on.

Skilled as he was at woodworking, his creativity didn't stop there. He was naturally curious and inventive, interested in how things worked now and how they could work even better in the future. Like all born inventors, he had a passion for improving things.

During the war, for example, folks began using a form of margarine called Oleo in place of butter, which was very expensive. Packaged in a one-pound plastic bag, Oleo started out as white but came with a small disc of yellow dye. The dye fixed Oleo's color, but the result was a large bowl of the butter-looking concoction. While that was better, it was still not very appealing.

There had to be a better way, Daddy decided. So he started making "butter molds." These wooden boxes had a hole in the top and a free floating bottom. The bottom piece was attached to a round peg which went through the hole in the top and acted as a plunger. You put your colored Oleo in the mold and placed it in the refrigerator. Once it hardened, you pushed the plunger, ending up with a yellow block that looked satisfyingly similar to an actual block of butter. I was too young to remember the details, but I've been told that Daddy's butter molds were sold and shipped from Miami to Seattle.

Eventually, my father and Granddaddy Keeton opened a wood-working manufacturing company that took up most of a city block on Monument Street. There they made butter molds, mantels, and custom-made furniture and cabinets. This enterprise thrived until the end of the war, when the availability of prefabricated furniture and cabinets dried up its business. About the only thing Daddy could find to do after that was sales. Over the years he sold stocks, bonds, hearing aids, automobile polish, tire-handling equipment, and picture frame supplies. Though he was usually home for the weekends, his sales work kept him mostly on the road. Sometimes he would be gone for two or even three weeks at a time. Daddy hated the traveling, and we hated having him gone. But along the way, he gained knowledge about a lot of different things, and that experience eventually led to several inventions.

While selling tire-handling equipment, for example, he worked with pneumatic machines used to separate truck tires from their wheels. As he watched the powerful pistons come out of the cylinders driven by air pressure, he got an idea.

At that time, tires were thinner and of poorer quality than they are today. Flat tires were a very frequent occurrence. (Once, when driving from Peoria, Illinois, to Jackson, Mississippi, I had four flats in a single day.) Flats were usually fixed by service stations. A hand jack had to be wheeled under the car's steel bumper and pumped up to change the tire or fix a flat. Daddy realized that an air cylinder could be used to make the process virtually effortless. Developing his new jack was neither as quick nor as easy as he first imagined, but Daddy finally sold the idea to Branick Manufacturing Co. in Fargo, North Dakota. Though he got a patent on it, he was a neophyte and did not do nearly as well as he should have from the invention. In the end, he sold the idea to Branick for $500 and a 5 percent commission, payable for only five years and only on the jacks sold in the U.S. Daddy gave the entire $500 to Fondren Presbyterian Church, explaining that it was during church that he got most of his ideas. I am not sure the preacher would see this as a compliment, but I am sure they were glad of the money.

By 1955, Daddy had decided he had to get off the road. Deciding to put his woodworking skills to good use, he and Mama opened a picture framing shop. This was a huge step, requiring them to sink everything they had and all the money they could borrow. In the beginning, Daddy had to continue to travel during the week, just to make ends meet. Mama was left alone all day every day to run the store and advise people on their choices of frame and mat.

Daddy knew a lot about woodworking, but little about the picture framing business. Mama had no knowledge about picture framing, much less about running a business. With three children at home (one requiring special attention) and no one to relieve her for lunch or help with questions, it must have been not only scary but lonely. I think this new venture took more guts for her than for Daddy. He seemed to be the more dynamic force, but Mama was the spark that kept him going and the glue that kept everything together. Somehow she ran the shop, did the grocery shopping, kept the house, and always had supper on the table at 6 p.m. Looking back, I can't imagine how she did it. At the time, totally wrapped up in my high school concerns, it never once occurred to me how much stress she and Daddy were experiencing in those years.

Each week when he came home from the road, Daddy went straight back to work, doing all of the framing that had been ordered the previous week. These were hard times for both of my parents, but neither complained. They just did what had to be done.

Picture framing was in its infancy when they opened their shop. Frames were still made by using a hand saw and miter box. The length of the frame was measured and marked, each piece carefully cut, and the frame glued together. The glass and the cardboard that served as backing also had to be measured and cut. All of this was painstaking and labor-intensive work, full of possibilities for minor mistakes that wasted both time and materials.

Naturally, Daddy immediately had ideas on how to improve the process. First, he set up a power radial arm saw to replace the miter box and handsaw. Then he connected up a vacuum to remove the dust. By embedding a ruler into the workbench, he could measure and cut the molding in one step; by building a sliding stop into it, he avoided having to measure each new piece separately.

The cutting of the cardboard was his next focus. He invented a wall-mounted cutter that would accept a large piece of cardboard, again with embedded rulers to make measuring easier. Using his knowledge of air cylinders (he really had a "thing" for air), he installed one cylinder to clamp the cardboard in place and another to cut it.

At this time, the beveled edges of picture frame mats were cut freehand. Daddy was skilled enough to master this art, but most framers and would-be framers weren't so deft. Daddy decided he wanted to invent a machine that anyone could use to cut a perfect mat with minimal practice.

Undoubtedly, this was the most frustrating project he ever attempted. He worked and worked on it, sometimes becoming so frustrated he would pick the machine-in-progress up, throw it against the wall, cuss a little, and bark, "This is impossible! I'm an *idiot* for wasting so much time on it!" Though he would often storm off in a huff, he would always return, more determined than ever to get it right.

Finally, the mat cutter was perfected. Daddy filed for a patent under the name Keeton Kutter and had twelve of the devices made up by the local machine shop. Still traveling at this time, he put all twelve in the trunk of the car and began calling on frame shops to demonstrate them. Once the trunk was empty, he would have twelve more made and start all over again. From this humble beginning, Keeton Kutters eventually spread worldwide. I know of frame shops that still used his original Keeton Kutter fifty years later, an enduring testament to his ingenuity.

In recognition of his work, my father was asked to be the first president of the newly formed Professional Picture Framers of America. Writing articles for the quarterly publication and giving talks around the country made him very nervous at first, but soon he did both with ease. For his first speech as president of the organization, he prepared his notes on a pile of 3" X 5" cards. After fumbling around with the cards at the beginning of his talk, he tossed them aside. "To hell with it," he said, "I'm just gonna talk to you like you are my next door neighbor." From that day on, he always spoke from the heart.

Daddy believed that much more could be gained by framers working together and sharing the secrets of the trade than by being secretive or competitive. He went all over the country trying to convince picture framers to agree, and was convincing enough that he took the organization to prominence. In addition to gaining national recognition, in May 1974 he was the first non-Englishman to be asked to address the Fine Art Trade Guild in London, England.

My father soon began manufacturing the many products he invented and developed for the picture framing business. He sold Keeton Picture Framing in 1979 to devote all of his time to manufacturing. Over the years the business earned my parents nice homes and new Cadillacs every year.

By the time my parents retired and moved to Florida, Daddy was happy just having a small ranch house, a small station wagon that he could use to haul lumber, and a fully equipped garage workshop. He never did get around to putting cars in his garages. They were always full of saws, lathes, drill presses, shapers, sanders, and things he'd seen in the latest shop catalogs. In his later years, Daddy devoted all of his time to woodworking projects. Still a believer in sharing knowledge and talent, he formed the Florida Woodworkers Association, hosting their regular meetings in his well-stocked garage workshop.

My father's success would have been remarkable for anyone, but was even more so for a man without a college education who had worked two jobs and struggled for every nickel. Thanks to the role model my parents provided and their hard work, I enjoyed the opportunities provided by not just college but also medical school. The older I get, the more I appreciate the remarkable things they accomplished, all without the same advantages they later gave me.

Afterword II:

Learning from Lee Lott

*A*FTER THE TIME DESCRIBED IN THE CLARENCE LEE LOTT JR. chapter, I lost touch with Lee. After three years of college I returned to Jackson to go to medical school, while Lee went into the Army. We didn't reconnect until 2007, when I attended graduation exercises at the Darlington School in Rome, Georgia. While reading the program, I noticed the name of Victoria Lee Lott from Jackson, Mississippi. I knew there had to be some connection to my old friend Lee.

I searched the audience, but didn't see him. When I called information for Lee Lott in Jackson, I was connected to Lee's son, Clarence Lee Lott III, who told me that his father was in fact there for his daughter Victoria's graduation. I finally found Victoria, who led me to Lee and his beautiful wife, Nina. Lee and I hadn't seen each other for over thirty years by then, but it was like we had only been apart for a few weeks. After a delightful visit, we agreed to get together. Unfortunately, we failed do so.

On July 4th a couple of years later, I was riding on a boat on Lake Cavalier, just north of Jackson. Dee was standing on the front of the boat dressed as the Statue of Liberty; my cousin Jimmy Keeton and his wife, Jona, who owned the boat, were with us as well. Lee was sitting on the dock at his lake house, playing with a new puppy. We visited for a few minutes and again agreed that we needed to get together. But again we failed to follow through, letting the 450 miles between us and our busy lives keep us apart.

In October 2010, I received a call from my cousin, Jimmy Keeton, who was Dean of the University of Mississippi Medical School. Jimmy told me that Lee had been involved in an automobile accident that left him paralyzed from the neck down and was facing surgery to stabilize his broken neck. I well knew the risks involved with this type of surgery. I told Jimmy that if Lee survived the operation and was in sufficiently good condition for visitors, I would come by to see him on my way to Oxford that weekend.

Happily, Lee did survive the surgery. He was awake and totally coherent when I saw him a few days later. I had been dreading the visit, wondering what words of encouragement, advice, or consolation I could offer him. To my mind, his was the worst possible situation a human being could face: one in which you are totally dependent on others, unable to control anything, including your own bodily functions. I thought that Lee would be morbidly depressed. I wasn't sure how I would deal with that, or how I could possibly help him.

When I arrived at the hospital, however, Lee was awake, alert, and cheerful—just like the Lee I had always known. In no time we were laughing and telling jokes. I would assure him that he was the still the ugliest person I had ever known; he would insist that as long as I was alive, he would never have to worry about that title.

I stayed with him an hour or so that first night and several hours the next morning. As an anesthesiologist, I often spent 24 hours or even longer working nonstop in a hospital, doing physically and mentally exhausting procedures and taking care of very sick patients. However, sitting in a hospital room with a friend or relative had always been difficult for me. It always reminded me of being five years old and trying to sit still through a church service. To my surprise, staying with Lee was never a problem, even on a couple of occasions when I was with him for close to eight hours. I enjoyed every moment I was with him. In fact, it felt like he was there to entertain *me*.

I made three trips to Jackson to visit Lee, and we had good times together on each. Each time I asked what I could bring him. He always requested a hamburger and milkshake from Brent's Drugs.

Was I ever glad to oblige! First, I would have done my best to get Lee something from the moon if that was what he wanted. Brent's Drugs was close and easy to get to. I had spent a considerable amount of my life there. It was across the street from Duling, my elementary school, as well as the Fondren Presbyterian Church. After school, Brent's was as packed as the exit ramp at the Ole Miss/Mississippi State football game. Even on Sunday mornings it was crowded, since both kids and adults went to Brent's between Sunday school and church.

Second, asking me to go to Brent's Drugs was like throwing Brer Rabbit into the briar patch. Brent's just happened to have the world's best chocolate malts and milk shakes.

You understand, I was only going to Brent's for Lee. But to ensure that Lee wouldn't feel uncomfortable, I would always order a malt for me too. In hindsight, I wouldn't be at all surprised if Lee didn't request his burger and malt more for my pleasure than his own.

Lee never once asked "Why me?" Nor did I even once hear him complain about anything. He remained happy, cordial, and friendly to everyone who entered his room. He was interested in them, their families, and their plans for the future.

I once asked him, "Lee, how are you doing?"

"I'm doing fine," he said.

"No," I said. "I mean how are you *really* doing?"

He was very quiet for a long minute or so, then looked me straight in the eye. "Well, I've got a real dogshit situation here," he told me. "I try not to think about it. I especially try not to think about my future. What bothers me most is thinking about Nina and my children."

I learned a lot from Lee during these visits. Lee's example taught me about life, about death, and about being happy in the face of genuine adversity. Many people, including spiritual gurus of all sorts, talk about living "in the now." They emphasize that the past is gone and unchangeable and the future is guaranteed to no one. They insist that all any of us ever have is the present moment. That sure sounds great, and of course, they're right. But I 've known very few people who actually lived according to those principles. After his accident, Lee Lott did. He never said so explicitly, but I think that Lee had truly learned to live fully in the moment, without regard to either the future or the past. I think he had decided he would be happy in the present, and to heck with everything else.

I am deeply grateful to have reconnected with Lee. As I said earlier, when I first went to see him in the hospital, I hoped to be able to help him in some way. As it turned out, he was the teacher and I was the student. I had a doctorate degree and several decades of experience, but I still had a lot to learn.

I was blessed to have had this time with him and to get to know his lovely wife, Nina, and his mother-in-law, Hazel, who are two of the most remarkable people I have ever met. His sister-in-law, Kim, his lovely daughters Olivia and Victoria and his sons Lee and Brad, are very special people as well.

Mr. & Mrs. Lott would have been proud of Lee and his family. I know I am.

Thank you, Lee. You taught me a lot, from the moment we met until the day you died.

Acknowledgements

Like most authors, I am indebted to many people for their help during the creation of this book. I am appreciative of Cathy House, CRNA, who was always encouraging. She collected stories I had written and forgotten and later gave them to me in a loose-leaf binder. Charles Alexander, a classmate from Murrah High School, actually wrote stories for me during my freshman English class, when the mere thought of writing was totally intimidating. I don't know why I did not think to ask him to write this book. It would have been a lot easier for me, and probably a lot better for you readers.

I am appreciative of all my family and friends who have offered their support, including those who told me not to quit my day job. Dr. George Sessions—my partner, mentor, good friend and editor—has taught me a great deal not only about writing, but about life in general. Mary Catherine St Louis offered both help and encouragement. Marty Ward, the No BS Business Coach, helped me see that while Billy was extremely mischievous, he was actually a good little kid with a big heart. She then nudged (okay, pushed) me into having these stories reviewed by a professional to see if they were worthy of printing. Lana McAra rendered that opinion as well as offering her encouragement.

Mim Esinberg acted as a delightful editor with a warm sense of humor and an abundance of red ink. Judy Parker, Dr. Robert Leonard, Dick Wilson, Dr. Donald Hall, Linda Brasfield Jordan, and Nina Lott all offered wisdom, support and encouragement.

Though I hope this book itself has shown my gratitude, I can't fail to acknowledge here all of the Fondrens: everyone and everything associated with the Big House and all its wonderful memories. Memories still dwell not only in our hearts, but also in the hearts of all of those that came along after the Big House was gone, through the lingering stories of our version of Camelot. I must also thank my Keeton grandparents and my great-grandfather, Daddy Bogue. While their home and lives were very different from those of my Fondren grandparents, they played a very significant part in my life as a child, and I will always be grateful.

I owe special thanks to my cousin Reverend Ken Goodrich, also an author, and one who greatly honored me by writing his version of many of these stories. When I asked Ken to write the Foreword for this book, he said no. However, he offered to write a Forewarning, instead—entirely the right approach to this material.

Additionally, I want to thank cj Madigan of Shoebox Stories, who designed this book with consummate professionalism, a sure eye, and a welcome enthusiasm for Fondren and Keeton family pictures.

Last in this list of contributors to the creation of this book, but certainly by no means least, my thanks go to author and book strategist Suzanne Fox, a remarkable lady of too many talents to mention. Like Mim Eisenberg, Suzanne too had an ample supply of red ink—I'm not sure why I keep getting that kind of editor. In addition, she had an ample supply of patience, wit, eloquence, tough love, and ability to read what I meant to say rather than what I actually wrote; this book is much closer to my intended meaning, and has many fewer exclamation points and capitalized phrases, thanks to her help. Suzanne has done a great job considering the little with which she had to work. I know her only by her voice on the phone, but consider her a very good friend.

All of us who grew up in and around Fondren appreciate the efforts of the Fondren Renaissance Foundation (http://www.fondren.org) and Find It In Fondren (http://www.finditinfondren.com), both of which have done an excellent job in publicizing and sustaining the uniqueness of the area. I must also acknowledge the contributions to my life of the Fondren Presbyterian Church; the Duling School; Bailey Junior High School; Murrah High School, particularly the Class of '58; and the University of Mississippi—or, as it is better known, Ole Miss. Though in ways different from these august institutions, the Boy Scouts, Brent's Drug Store, and the Pix Theater were also formative in my development.

To all of those that I have failed to mention: please know that the lapse is due not to my lack of appreciation, but rather to my aging memory. Please forgive me, as all of the Fondrens and many others have always had to do.

Photo Captions & Credits